In Wild Waters

IN WILD WATERS

JOHN BAILEY

Chris Turnbull

J Bailey

The Crowood Press

First published in 1989 by
The Crowood Press
Ramsbury, Marlborough
Wiltshire SN8 2HE

British Library Cataloguing in Publication Data

Bailey, John
  In wild waters.
  1. Great Britain. Angling
  I. Title
  799.1'2'0941

ISBN 1-85223-092-4

Acknowledgements
Photographs by John Bailey, Sharon Bailey,
Roger Miller and John MacDonald.
Line drawings by Chris Turnbull

Typeset by Photosetting & Secretarial Services, Yeovil
Printed in Great Britain by Butler & Tanner Ltd, Frome

Contents

Introduction

Christmas Night at the Flyfisher's Lake

It was 25 December 1986. The day broke wet with wind from the west. I fished a very dark dawn at the Flyfisher's Lake till late morning without seeing a pike, or come to that, any other angler or human being. I left, only to return five hours later. I could not keep away. I knew the gully that I was fishing was frequented by a monster pike as the sun set and darkness crept in. I had seen him two days earlier, gleaming ivory in my torch beam, a foot beneath the lake surface that was crinkling into ice.

So, that Christmas Day, darkness fell. The stars were out, the wind had died and the night was perfectly still. The whole Norfolk countryside slept. Christmas night and people everywhere were home and the valley showed no signs of the usual headlights on the highroad. I was as totally alone as I had been on that day's lonesome dawn, just watching floats, thinking of monsters, dreaming of Christmas giants. At one point, the live baits began to panic and took both floats, dipping and weaving out of the torch beam. I checked my net and prepared for action – but all in vain – whatever had cruised by the little fish had gone on its way and the night settled back, peaceful again. It was at around six o'clock that my thoughts began to wander, as they do for all of us when the night seems endless and without hope of action.

A Salmon from Exmoor

I went back to a day in early September when many fishing truths had seemed to come together. It was, at least until then, one of the best days of my angling life. The setting was an Exmoor valley, wherein runs a tantalisingly beautiful river. Most of the year the water holds little more than trout of a few ounces in weight. In times of spate, however, the stream hosts a salmon run and so it was this particular week.

The line zipped tight.

The silver grilse, fresh from the seas, stitched their way past from pool to pool. So it was, they pulled me out dusk after dawn. This particular dawn had been mildly grey. Salmon had sploshed their way up river. Once one rolled, bream-like, over the fly. Once one nipped at the tinsel and feather and finally I lost one after ten seconds as it hurtled like starlight over the lip of a pool into rapids and salvation beneath.

Morning opened out. With two dogs I set off up the valley to the next village four miles distant. It was a lovely trail through forest and unbroken pasture, rising steeply all the while. At each pool I watched for salmon, marking their lie and my fishing position upon return. The dogs flushed out rabbits. Hawks hung above in the ever blueing sky. We rested at the Willow Pool pub. I slept a while on a south-facing slope and pressed back down as the shadows first appeared on the valley side. I fished for every salmon that I had marked on the uphill climb. I stirred one or two fish from their position. They wavered in the current, gleams of ivory, hesitating over the lure in front of them. But always they relaxed back to their original positions.

The final net.

The last pool came. It was the tiniest. It was surrounded by trees and faced by a scree. I eased into its neck and fished very tightly down through the water. The last cast came and went. Nothing. I trudged out and stroked the dogs. It was no matter. It had been a wonderful day. As I turned, five yards from me, a grilse came out. I did not see the fish. It was the roar of its re-entry that brought me back to the waterside. Again I cast. At once the line zipped tight. That miracle of creation was on the end of my line and a firework fight began. No matter what the fish tried I would not let it leave the pool and lose me in the white water. He jumped nine times, then ten and even eleven. He was bird, not fish – wing, not fin. All the while he fought no more than a rod's length from me. I saw his silver glint over and over in the last of the evening light and finally my little wing hit its final net. The dogs crowded round to see him. A buzzard mewed. A knot of deer appeared on the skyline waiting for dusk to come down and drink. The sheen of the salmon turned from ivory to amber in the softening light and at once all the combinations of my life slipped and slid together to open a safe of wonders. Utter satisfaction was mine.

The walk back down the valley was inspirational – not just a last light on the oaks or the ever singing river beneath me nor the silvery sheen, the fresh-run salmon, the pearl of nature, swinging at my side – it was more what he represented that was important.

In truth, he was the reason I was there, by the pike lake, that Christmas, when everyone else was with their families. I wanted a pike unscarred, uncaught, fresh, wild and as beautiful as nature intended. Because all pike at the Lake are removed, I knew the water could give me this, and any other pike that pulled my float down between now and Boxing Day morning had been neither caught, touched, or probably seen by any man. There would be no name to this pike, nor tag. No history but her private story since the egg. And somehow, that night, I decided that this was how I wanted my fishing to be for a while – at least as far as is possible in these crowded days and islands of ours.

I wanted fish with the freshness still about them and have no man tell me their weight before they even hit the sling. It would not be easy, I knew, but I resolved to travel a little and perhaps hit on fish others had not tried for. I would break away, have a few adventures and see what I could do. All in all, I thought that Christmas night that my fishing had never looked to be more exciting. And I could not have been more right. But, of course, what follows is not simply a succession of tales of big fish won or lost or never even contacted at all. Events occurred along the way far too bizarre to ignore and anyway to do so would pervert the spirit of what happened, some of which was even pure farce. Nor do I want to give the impression of battling alone against the elements and unseen monsters. That too would be utterly incorrect for I had some stout helpers along

A pearl of nature.

Satisfaction was mine.

The silvery sheen at my side.

the way. There was Roger Miller of course, better known, when the alcohol flows, as Line Singer. Now, really, here is a friend and a damn good fisherman too. And, talking of alcohol leads straight to Reel Screamer – friend, drinker, novice, adventurer, talker and trier all. Mr Christopher Yates and a certain Bob 'Breeks' James made an appearance, dropping in from their particular time warp of split cane, centre pins and fob watches. They departed again aghast at what the present holds! Norrie, the giant builder and angler from Edinburgh, who kept me sane and safe in a certain northern house of ill repute was there, and I will have to introduce Tarus Bulba – if only to persuade you never to go to Wales! There were some lovely older anglers like Billy Giles. There was an absolute liar and there was even a ghost. There was, I am afraid, rather a lack of ladies, which, believe me, Reel Screamer regretted! We did have one rather special encounter with some once, but, perhaps that is it: if you go fishing often enough with such a crew you are likely to see everything sooner or later.

1

Piking at the Flyfisher's Lake

When I joined the Flyfisher's it was quite specifically for the trout fishing and I had little thought of piking in the few days that this was permissible. However, my first winter there, Chris Turnbull talked me into a session and I was pleased to welcome him along as my guest. I remember a raw day on the big pit, with the wind driving in from the south west towards the Clubhouse bank. I certainly remember Dan Leary, that great old warrior of Norfolk angling, was there but, apart from him, there were few other men out on the water that day.

I knew that my heart wasn't in the job at all. The club policy of catching and removing pike disheartened me. So many had been removed that I really couldn't believe many – or any – big fish remained there. Chris fished a sardine and I a herring and we sat runless until a weary half light and I persuaded Chris to leave. I don't believe anyone caught a thing that day and I was damned pleased to be in the car and on the way home.

A couple of days passed and I was due to meet Robbie, the Flyfisher's Lake secretary, on a local river to mend some groynes.

'Dan had a big one yesterday,' Robbie said on the way through the wood. Oh God, I thought. 'How big?' I asked.

'Guess.' I hated that but I began. 'Twenty?' 'More.' 'Twenty five?' 'Up again.' This was getting nightmarish. 'Thirty?' 'Again.' 'Thirty five?' I said through clenched teeth. I dreaded the response! 'Up.' 'Thirty-seven?' 'Still more!' I grasped the nettle and with a groan I said 'Forty?' 'Thirty-nine and a half pounds when weighed! We guessed it was probably a Forty when caught!'

It was a brilliant, fresh, unmarked fish and I vowed then never to miss a Flyfisher's open day unless death intervened and I don't think that I have done . . . hardly. Of course, Dan deserved his fish, because the Flyfisher's is a killer of a place. It has broken some and many won't even start there. Dan's incredible fish died, alas, and he had the great pike set up. I went to admire the quite wonderful piece of work.

40lb when caught?

'It could have weighed more,' Dan said. 'It was quite empty but for one sardine!'

Of course this was not the first great pike from the water. A few years before Reg Sandys had taken his own thirty pounder from the Lake. In days to come I was to catch a thirty-six pounder and Jim Tyree a thirty-two pounder. And yet, I *knew* for sure that the water could produce pike still larger! There could be no wonder that my pike fishing there was charged with electricity. Any Optonic shrill, any plop of a disappearing float, could well herald history in the making.

Preparation for a Stay at the Flyfisher's Lake

The preparation by the lakeside the day before the fishing begins is all part of the excitement. Miller and I are like kids at a party. It is part of the joy to get down to the water in the early afternoon and spend two or three hours putting together everything that we are likely to need for the next week or so. After all we will be there solidly, virtually living there in cold, darkest winter. We feel it is imperative to have everything sorted out and ready to go.

Firstly, we make up our battery of rods. We put up two long rods for drifting. I cannot over-emphasise how useful a technique drifting is. We must be ready for any good wind so as to be able to cover more water and previously untouched pike. We also assemble two very strong rods of test curves approaching three pounds. We use these for casting dead baits at a long range. We will put a heavy bomb near the hooks and possibly pack a dead bait with polystyrene and make it float enticingly off the bottom. Finally we prepare four more standard rod set-ups. These are for fishing closer into the bank. We generally settle in a deep gully and like to have our live baits fished float paternoster in the ten- to fifteen-foot water. It is with real satisfaction that we view our eight rods leaning against the Clubhouse ready to be used in the coming week.

Obviously, all the lines on the rods are brand, spanking new. We use fifteen-pound line. This may seem excessive but we do not think so. The need is always there for the strongest, practical line strength. This is especially so when drifting. To bring a big fish back over innumerable gravel bars plays havoc with a line and can easily lose you a big fish. I well remember the case of a 'mere' eighteen pounder that was hooked on the drift. The fight was sensational. It plugged away spinning the reel handle as it went. Some two hundred or more yards out it hit a snag and Miller and I had to get into the boat, row out and free it. The line was almost gone. It was frayed and shredded to a mere two pounds breaking strength. We take similar care with our traces. Every one is new twenty-pound test. Every one is checked each cast.

A 'mere' 18lb.

For hooks we use the strongest we can find and we admit that we tend to go against the normal trend liking barbed hooks. Our favourite has often been Eagle Claws. We do really feel, with the hard fight these fish give, barbs give us a better chance of landing a pike at the end. We pride ourselves on our skill at unhooking our fish. Miller especially is an expert surgeon, as his scarred hands will testify. Certainly we like to think that by using barbed hooks we've never hurt a fish yet at the Flyfisher's Lake. It does not pay to be dogmatic with hooks, however. After all, did not Jim Tyree's fish come on a *single* size four!

Our landing nets are large. Our keep sacks are the best available. We take massive care with our clothing. For me a one-piece thermal suit is an absolute necessity. It is also good to have a couple of umbrellas ranged on the bank as shelter from rain, cold, and winds.

Our baits are now ready with us. We do use dead baits though we have little confidence in them. We have them prepared but prefer freshwater baits, particularly roach, carp and trout. We do take sea baits and Miller once, for example, did have an eleven-pound fish on a smelt. In short we do not like to leave anything at all to chance. For our 'lives' we like to use trout. These must be caught from surrounding streams so as not to break the laws of the water authority in our region.

Finally, all the extras have to be taken into account. Miller in particular does need to consume a steady supply of food so stocks have got to be prepared. Me? I am more of a drinking man and a few tipples have to be at hand. And, remember, we are virtually spending Christmas at the water. One year we brought a Christmas tree, complete with balloons, into the Clubhouse! I think the other members thought we were totally mad and since then we have been rather ashamed and stopped that particular little nicety!

And so we leave as the sun sets. There are only a few hours of darkness to go before the big 'off'. We lock everything away in the Clubhouse and drive away down the track, secure in the knowledge that our preparation has been quite as good as anybody could make it. Now all we have to do is to set the alarms for three o'clock but I know that we are hardly able to sleep with the anticipation and excitement of the coming week in our minds.

Thoughts on Bait

The question of bait does interest me. Undoubtedly, these great, clear-water pike are sight feeders and live baits almost always outscore deads. Very probably, pike prefer to feed on live fish and are only forced to take deads in murky waters where they cannot see to hunt. So far, so good. Obviously, the water where visibility is ten, fifteen, twenty, any number of feet in fact, is a great help to the sight feeder, the hunter of live fish. But what of the prey? It, too, can quite as easily see the coming of the predator and make a very spirited attempt at escape...

Miller and I float paternostered seven- to eight-inch trout. We had them swimming normally between five and ten feet in water that varied between twelve and fourteen feet. On several occasions we have had line streaming from the clips and off the spool in carp-style ten-yard runs. Then the float would reappear. The trout, on being reeled in, would be unmarked. Very possibly a marauder had been outstripped by a small fish pulling some thirty to fifty yards of line, a bung and a two-/three-ounce lead. On two astonishing dawn occasions our trout surfaced and swam in agitated circles before being attacked in the most explosive of fashions by obviously very large fish. Both times the pike missed its mark and in alarm the trout returned to the bank by our feet, again unscathed.

Even when the pike does make its attack and succeeds in grasping a lively trout, a terrific underwater battle must follow. Hooking a trout on, even wearing gloves, is difficult and I am not at all sure the pikes' famed gripping teeth clench as vice-like as legend would suggest. If the trout has become agitated, the float will dive, hang sub-surface for fifteen to thirty seconds, re-emerge and the trout bait will power out of the zone. Later, huge scars and punctures will be in evidence on the fish. Had the pike attacked and let go? Had its spirited dinner won a reprieve?

The awareness of the stock-bred trout of danger is immediately evident. Agitation, often extreme, nearly always heralds a take. Trout, ten or even fifteen yards away seem able to sense the presence of an active predator. All this would make it appear that dead fish would be the easier target – especially in artificially stocked trout waters where over-wintering casualties are of significant numbers. What could be more tempting than the drifting, recently dead three pound brown trout to a thirty pound plus pike? Some of these dead or dying fish perhaps do go down the gullets of pike but not, I suspect, a great many. Indeed, after five years of fishing – generally with an equal ratio of live to dead baits – only five runs have come to the deads. Three were dropped. One drifted smelt produced an eleven pounder. One pound trout halved produced true drama...

The date was 22 December 1984. The dead trout lay in the neck of a deep gully thirty yards from the southern bank. Nothing had happened since dawn but at 10.30 a.m. the float above it steamed against the wind and submerged. The line snaked out. A strong strike produced an alarming curve from an obviously large fish that simply held bottom the way the big pike do. After some seconds, perhaps a minute, it began a slow but ponderously unstoppable run down the

The typical barrel-shaped trout water pike.

gully. Then the hooks pulled clear and that seemed an end to the whole business. Not quite. Twenty yards down the deep channel a huge flat appeared on the wind chopped surface. It spread out to become the size of a large motor car of perfectly calm water. Then another . . . a third . . . a fourth . . .until like four huge stepping stones down the wind lane, these flats marked the flight path of the escaping giant.

If dead baits are slow business, and a lively six-inch trout can often evade capture to cause annoyance, the case for a more feeble bait is overwhelming. Roach, bream, dace and perch all fall into this category, but the environmental case against using indigenous fish is strong. Smaller trout, tired trout, or better, tethered trout could be the answer I suspect. Still, there are always the occasions when a small roach can prove attractive to both the pike and therefore the pike angler.

The Villain's Tale

When some of us began to wonder if the trout that we were using for bait were too lively for the pike that were chasing them, we decided to try smaller, weaker, coarse fish in their place. In the midst of a very cold winter acquiring such fish was bound to be a problem. However, one of our number did have one lake in mind as a last resort if things should come to it. They did, and he, the Villain, went. Now, let me say here at once that none of us like using wild fish for bait and would never do so if it were taking a man's sport. The lake was, however, a carp syndicate and the multitude of stunted roach were merely a nuisance there. We realised that one of our number, the Villain, was also breaking bylaws which we too regretted.

The problems did not end for the Villain here though. Not only did the fish have to be caught, but they also had to be got away under the nose of the ferociously aggressive owner who lived on the water itself. The Villain's plan was a good one: a dustbin of water was stationed half a mile away in a field. The roach, if and when caught, would be put in a wetted sack and simply carried in the creel to the van and to the bin. The roach would be out of the water for no more than three or four minutes and with temperatures near zero should come to little harm.

Fishing commenced in the small, shallow, clear lake covered with cat ice. Bites were not plentiful but a net began to build up. The muscular owner came over to inspect, suspicious no doubt as to why a big fish man should freeze his monkey climbers off for roach of barely three inches! Still, civilities were exchanged and the fishing continued. Twenty roach in the net and the Villain began to pack, quite aware of the hawk eye checking his every move from the window across the water. The keep net was hauled ashore and the Villain made every attempt to look excited as he fell to the ground, shielding the fish from the owner's view. In a trice they were in the sack and in the bag! Then, with great display, the net was resubmerged and the play of returning the roach was successfully enacted.

Gear slung on shoulder, with brisk strides the Villain made it successfully to the van and rattled away down the lane to the field where the bin waited. He got out, lifted up the sack of fish and ran like a ferret across the meadow. He rounded the hedge and came face to face with two horsewomen – one of them the fishery owner's wife – prancing round and round the bin.

'Is this yours?' she asked. Obviously it was and the Villain had to think quickly. 'Yes, indeed it is,' he replied.

'But it's full of water!'

'Yes, I know.'

'But why ever?'

Inspiration had to hit the Villain quickly. 'The van. You see the radiator leaks so I keep supplies here and there to help me out.'

'You mean to say, all along your usual routes there are dustbins half full of water!'

'Yep – that way I don't blow up the engine. So, if you'll excuse me I'll dash. I can smell the damned thing burning from here.'

The roach all lived. The Villain received a hero's welcome and the horsewoman thought him a very strange young man indeed.

The Mystery of Moved Fish

Sadly, all pike caught from the Flyfisher's Lake have to be moved or killed. I feel that this is a tragedy when it comes to the big fish in particular. Any pike in the teens of pounds or over is a sensational creature and here, particularly so. I have never seen shorter, firmer, more muscular pike and their colouring is simply superb. Believe me, their tummies are like snow!

It is also my belief – or rather now accepted biological fact – that big pike tend to eat small pike in preference to trout. They are, simply, easier to catch and no predator exerts more energy than need be. I believe that most of the members would agree jack pike are on the increase and it is these little scamps that do the real damage, snipping and tearing at trout, often unable to kill. Nobody wishes to see wounded trout with gaping intestines, but the removal goes on.

Most fish are transported to an adjoining pit, far smaller and well muddied, called the Murky. There is a good head of bream and roach in the Murky so the transfer should not be any type of death sentence. And yet, the vast majority of these pike disappear, never to be caught again. Of course, some are seen again, but these are in the minority. It is quite probable some of the fish die. Pike handling is not what it might be in all instances by what are, after all, flymen. Some pike do end up deep hooked. Traces and hooks have been left in. Blood on the banks has not been an uncommon sight. Even well handled, the trauma of the hooking, the playing and their removal has probably been too stressful for some older fish.

Yet, the question remains unanswered as to why so few big pike are found dead. One large body has turned up in recent times – but I believe that is all. Perhaps some have never risen to the surface. Perhaps others have rotted unnoticed in reed beds, but I do not feel death claims all these exiles.

A handful of large pike does get caught from the Murky. I remember for instance a twenty-six pounder caught by one member and a twenty-one-pound fish caught by me. Miller has had a twenty pounder. All these fish appeared in excellent condition but not as bulky as the lake pike. It could well be that these fish are larger ones which have gone back in weight. They have lived on but slimmed down to adapt to their environment. But this is not all the answer. Many recognisable big fish have never been seen again, for example, my thirty-six-pound pike and Jim Tyree's thirty-two-pound fish.

One friend suggested, quite seriously, that as the pits are so close together an underground (or should it be underwater?) passage links the two and the pike can swim through it to their old home. Why are there no trout in the Murky, for surely the passage must be two-way? I also recently noticed the level of the Murky to be a good few inches higher than that of the Flyfisher's Lake. If the two were linked, then that could not possibly happen. So, sadly, this romantic and optimistic theory cannot be the case.

Every fish that I have taken from the Murky has been a cautious one. Baits are picked up and dropped almost at once. Slicks appear on the surface where a bait has been shaken and rejected. Pike send bubbles up around a bait – tench-like in fact – but no run develops. When a strike is possible, the hooks often pull away in seconds and if a fish is actually landed then the hold is almost always precarious. Only by fishing the very best baits, with the most careful of presentations, have Miller and I done any good at all on the Murky. Increasingly, it is my belief that the majority of the pike live on in the Murky but that their single time capture has made them highly suspicious of bait and tackle. Of course, I know there are oft-caught pike, but perhaps they are mug fish or need anglers' baits.

This theory might well appear far fetched. After all, pike are not supposed to be the most intelligent of species. But then neither are tench. Yet, on opening

Bailey's 36lb pike.

day 1988, Miller and I were fishing a clear estate lake when a big tench came, head down and feeding hard, into the swim. We moved to our rods, expecting action. The tench inched two feet towards our floats, stopped, levelled up, looked straight at the gear and literally bolted! Not for eight or nine months had that tench seen tackle but it remembered and reacted. Carp are not the only wise fish: tench, and very probably pike, are not far behind them.

Nocturnal Feeding

On 1 December 1985 Norwich big fish angler Jim Tyree had a run of small pike. He then caught a sixteen pounder. He was delighted as it was his best pike ever up till that time. Twenty minutes later, sensationally, he doubled that record with a fabulous fish of thirty-two pounds. The time was approximately 3.20 p.m. In an hour of ceaseless action his piking world had been turned upside-down by this pack of fish moving through his swim. Miller and I were a little thoughtful, as, a while before Jim's action, we had experienced three dropped runs out in the bay to the left of him. It was our belief that the group of fish had passed us by, not yet feeding, so we camped for the night around Jim's position on the pontoon which is on the point of the bay.

With the coming of darkness, the lake emptied. I took my rod to Jim's position and cast out two live baits into the deep gully. I kept a torch beam alternating from the one float to the other. Then I had a little trouble with the battery. The beam came back and I found the right hand float quite easily. The left hand float, however, I could not find. The line was tight. I did not know how long the bait had been taken – perhaps a minute or more. I could not risk a deep hooking so I wound down and struck at once. Possibly that was my mistake – or at least fate had dealt me a bad hand, for the fish went out deep and slow into the open water. It was sullen, unstoppable, a truly big fish I knew, and then the hooks pulled free. It was past six in the evening, over two hours after sunset.

On 24 December 1987, it was a perfect night and we determined to stay on late, keen to cram in good fishing time when we could. Well into true darkness, the alarm sounded and a twenty-two-pound fish fought hard but came finally to the bank. To add to this pike, eleven and a half hours later, and still an hour before the new light of the Christmas Day, we took a second pike of just under the twenty pound mark.

Of course, there is nothing new in nocturnal feeding. It is mentioned, for example, in Buller's book on pike, and Bill Giles, then and now, remembers many night attacks in his long career. There could be many reasons for pike night feeding. Possibly, it is easier for them to approach their prey. Much of their prey

The coming of darkness.

The fruits of nocturnal fishing.

Miller with two beauties.

becomes more active at night, especially the bream and the roach, and pike, therefore, have adapted to this behaviour. Dusk and dawn are acknowledged as very good feeding times but perhaps we ought to extend this to cover true darkness. Certainly, our friend Nick Beardmore had excellent results on Norfolk's River Bure, fishing way into darkness, on even the coldest of winter nights. Certainly, the big fish on Flyfisher's Lake move way after the sun has set.

Water's Vitality

The ability of this water to sustain its flow of big fish is amazing. A thirty-nine pounder, thirty-six pounder, thirty-two pounder and thirty pounder have all been caught and removed. In six years, forty-seven more fish of fifteen pounds or over have also been taken and removed and yet very large pike still remain there. In the good weather of 1987, a twenty pounder a day was the rule but still the water is not worked out; several huge fish go unmolested.

On Christmas Day 1986, I was fishing alone, an hour after dark. Miller had left slightly earlier, a quite broken man after a run lost to a bite off. (We now use up wire traces when float paternostering.) The powerful torch beam was directed

Mottled perfection.

A Flyfisher's Lake monster.

onto float after float, each one lying only a rod's length from the bank in the deep gully that we so favour. Then it was that something to the left of the extreme bait caught the light and reflected it back in a large glow of dull silver. I turned the torch on to the object and in the gin-clear, becalmed water three pike emerged, swimming only a few inches beneath the Lake's surface. They were under the torchlight for some two minutes and at one stage were less than six feet from me. I was able to make quite exact impressions of their length from features along the bankside and my belief is that the smallest of the trio was around twenty pounds. The middle fish I put around the low/mid-thirties and the largest was between forty-nine and fifty-two inches long. Considering Dan Leary's thirty-nine-and-a-half-pound fish was forty-six inches in length, that final fish could well have been into the high forties – or beyond.

I returned, of course, before dawn after two more fruitless hours fishing. On the first cast I hooked and landed an eighteen and three-quarter pounder; could it possibly be that the triumvirate was still in the area? The trout live baits were active for over an hour and I expected the run of a lifetime at any moment. It was not to be; daylight grew stronger; the baits relaxed; whatever was prowling the gully had moved to an inaccessible area offshore. Still, as I write this, I know

Dawn breaks.

there is a very good chance that this most enigmatic of pike waters could hold one, if not two, massive pike.

The chemistry of big fish waters like this is fascinating. The size of the water is probably important. At twenty-odd acres it is, for lowland England, a largish water. The clarity seems to produce big fish of all species. Big bream, roach and tench all exist there. Perhaps the pellets that are introduced in large quantities for the stock trout in a pen help enrich the entire lake. Perhaps the constant culling of the pike stocks has some bearing on the ultimate size reached. Undoubtedly, the number of rainbow trout stocked every year as naive stew pond fish has some bearing. All evidence suggests that they are far easier prey than natural born roach or bream.

I also believe that limited fishing time is important. There are approximately eleven fishing days every year. It is quite possible for a fish to slip through the angler's net, as it were, for eight or nine years and grow extremely large. Indeed, compare this with a normal water where the pike season lasts for a good six months. There, a big fish of nine years old has four and a half years to evade anglers. It is more likely to be caught and perhaps to die from bad handling than here at the Flyfisher's Lake where a nine-year-old fish has only ninety-nine days to cope with. Of those, nine are Christmas days when hardly anybody is in the water. Also, on average, three or four days a year are useless due to weather conditions, so another thirty days are gone. A big fish at the Flyfisher's has only fifty days of its entire life during which to remain anonymous. Certainly, these are uncaught fish in fabulous condition. Glorious skin patterns and colours, whiteness of belly, freshness of mouth and fighting abilities testify to that. Reg Sandys' thirty pounder took over half an hour to land and gave runs of seventy or even eighty yards at times.

The amount of food in the pit is also desperately important. The lake has its normal population of roach and bream, but on top of this, seven thousand or more one to three pound trout are stocked annually. Four to five thousand are accounted for by the anglers. That leaves over two thousand fish, some of which die and rot but some of which, probably the majority, must go down the maws of pike. So the biomass of the Lake is immense. There are many bait fish going in. There are also many pike coming out. The equation is obvious. Very large pike are always a possibility at the Flyfisher's Lake.

No piking today.

One the pike will not get. Reg Sandys looks on.

The Law of Diminishing Returns

The big bay near the Clubhouse is the obvious area to fish and, indeed, is a place where most people settle. Most obviously the walk to it is minimal, but more importantly, it is the area to the north and east of the pit and therefore receives the majority of the winds. It is general pike lore that the windward shore is the most productive to fish. There is the added bonus of the trout pens also in this area. Occasional escapees must make the place attractive to pike. Also the daily introduction of pellets does tend to draw trout already in the lake.

On the bays of the vast Scottish and Irish lochs it has been noticed the sport has died after an initial glut. So too, in the infinitely smaller Flyfisher's Lake. In December 1987, for example, between twenty-five and thirty fish came in three days from the Clubhouse area. Good weather conditions continued and actually improved, but thereafter, the catches went down quickly. In a single week it seems that there was not time for new fish to filter in from the rest of the lake.

The enterprising angler therefore has two major alternatives. He can leave the Clubhouse area and go in search of fresh water to fish. This is made difficult by stringent club rules that disallow fishing from the major island area that commands the rest of the lake. The other possibility, if the wind is right, is to drift.

John Nunn capitalises on the central glut.

Roger Miller copes with the later, slower days!

Calvin Warnes with a 21lb fish
– the last big catch of the
December period.

Drifting is a most glorious method of pike fishing. It demands constant thought and action. The angler is playing with the wind as a man would play on the fiddle. It is quite possible to fish at over an eighth of a mile and the amount of water covered is, therefore, fantastic. It is exactly the method needed on sparsely stocked waters. I will not describe the method of drifting in detail as I have already done so in the book *Pike – the Predator becomes the Prey*. However, I will repeat one or two tips. This is a method that demands every part of the tackle to be perfect. The strain on gear at two or three hundred yards is immense. There is weed to cope with, gravel bars and the fight is very likely to be protracted. A long rod is almost essential. The line must be well greased. Breaking strains should not be less than twelve pounds. After each drift it pays to check the line quite carefully for any fraying or damage caused. Hooks must be needle sharp and binoculars are absolutely essential to watch the float closely once it exceeds eighty or ninety yards.

Certainly, the drift method gave me probably my most spectacular fishing memory – the capture of the 'thirty-six' from the Flyfisher's Lake. The take I will never forget. I have tried to measure it as best as I can and I guess the distance to be around one hundred and sixty yards. My binoculars were well trained on the big vain float in the morning light when it simply disappeared. A more complete vanishing act I have never witnessed. I felt it must be a fish but, of

A good wind and Bailey gets the drifts under way.

course, at that distance, with the method then new to me, I could not be absolutely sure. I remember, vividly, winding down to strike. It seemed an age before the line grew tight and I realised I was making contact. I wound down further until the rod began to take on its test curve and simply walked back up the bank. I moved five yards and everything was locked solid, my heart sank. Thirty seconds passed and my disappointment seemed confirmed. Only then, suddenly, did the rod buck. My heart leapt. The rod arched and jaggered down towards the water. At this immense range I was actually forced to give line!

I have mentioned the fight in *Pike – the Predator becomes the Prey*, but there were one or two incidents which were omitted and which have stayed with me. The first was when, at around eighty or ninety yards this great fish began a series of tail walks. My heart absolutely froze during those moments. The rings thus created were quite extraordinary. It must go down as one of the more astonishing sights of my fishing life. The second moment of great note was when, in the clear water, we (Jack the Fishery Manager and I), saw the fish circling some twenty-five yards out. I was astonished. At that time, more than anything, I wanted a twenty-five-pound-plus pike. I asked Jack whether he thought this fish would break that barrier. Jack simply nodded and said, 'Over thirty!' I knew he would be right. After all, he had been on the Thurne system during the great heydays of the 1950s and 1960s and he of all people knew a big fish when he saw one. The landing too was dramatic. The pike fell through the net. The hooks fell from its jaws. I only managed to grasp it at the last possible second. By then onlookers had gathered. I was asked what scales I had. I had with me the thirty-two-pound Avens and a man said they would not be powerful enough! I remembered the forty-four pound set in the bottom of the car. The same man shook his head and said again, 'Not powerful enough!' My God, I thought, perhaps I should send for Pickfords!

It seems then that during the latter part of the week at the Flyfisher's Lake when times get difficult, drifting is the best possible way of picking up fish. The other alternative is, of course, to fish at night when pike possibly begin to roam and feed more actively.

2

The Boathouse Lake

A Return

For many years, I had foolishly, conceitedly believed that I had already caught the largest carp that swam in the Boathouse Lake. The keeper told me so when he landed the fish for me, and I had believed him. As a result, I had rarely gone back, apart from to dangle awhile and bask in the complete beauty of the water. Quite what prompted me to ask for a week on the lake in 1987 I do not know. Most probably, I simply wanted to find a little peace, a little quiet and a little time. I saw the Boathouse Lake as my place, far from the madding crowd, where I could work sometimes, fish, sleep or stroll exactly as the mood decided to take me.

Late on an early summer afternoon, I walked down the meadow to the waterside to plan for the next day's start. Everything I saw was blissful, basking in warmth, overlaid by mellow sunlight. 'This is the place to be,' sighed the oaks, the beeches and I. I made no attempt at concealment or careful approach, but strolled right down to the lake's edge. I was taken aback to see the water so clear when before it had always been murky. The revelations had just begun.

After only yards, I saw a big carp lying quite calmly over a pure sand bottom. I dropped down to my knees, focused on it with the binoculars and examined its every scale. It was a very long, colourful fish, well into twenty pounds and obviously, I believed, the fish I had caught back in the 1979/80 season. I was overjoyed to see it still alive and so obviously well. Only after a long while did I move on and then with no real expectation of seeing more big fish.

At the far end of the lake a series of islands guards the shallows and it was there that my world was to be turned upside down. At first, of course, I knew the dark shapes had to be branches, fallen in during some winter storm, but even as I reached for the field-glasses the shapes were moving. I scanned an acre or so of the bay before me. Carp after carp lay in the sun-warmed shallows, as thickly

A Boathouse Lake wildie from early days.

and as huge as a fleet at anchor. I saw a dozen big fish. More. Fifteen. There was another one under the tree! There went a couple around the island! I had twenty big carp in front of me. Bless me, those glasses shook. All of them, I guessed, were twenty pound fish. A couple looked to be thirties perhaps and one incredible one I believed both then and since, to be bigger, much bigger than any carp I had seen clearly before.

I settled down behind a bush of elderflower and watched the fish until sundown. Then, as the rays filtered through the woodland behind, the fish moved in scatterings away into the main body of the lake. I remained there, however, pondering on what I had seen, mind and heart both racing, excited beyond belief, impatient for the next day when my permission began and I could get after those fabulous fish.

Dusk was well in when I walked out of the estate, down the track to my car. I met an estate worker walking his dog in the last of the light. I accompanied him to his cottage and we stood talking there as the bats flickered around the eaves and in and out of the solemn oaks. He had been on the estate man and boy. He knew everything about it for sixty years at least and he was a fund of knowledge on the Lake. This history of the last two hundred years was quite typical.

Built in the mid-eighteenth century, the lake had lain undisturbed until the Second World War. By then, however, it was deep in silt, thin in water and near the end of its life. Most landowners would have let it go – but not this one. He had it drained, let it stand to dry out and then got his horse teams on the job to plough away the silt and cart it out to fertilise the neighbouring fields. In the autumn of 1950 the rains began to fill the reborn lake once more and by the spring of 1951 it glittered with fresh, revitalised light. In June, or July perhaps (my informant could not quite remember), fifty or so yearling carp were stocked and that was an end to the matter as far as the estate was concerned. Its attention was directed elsewhere and the babies could now sink or swim as they chose. Quite apparently twenty or so at least had decided to swim!

I reached home about midnight and before going to bed read a little of B.B. at Wood Pool. I turned to that classic book *Redmire*. I read a little Walker, and finally I set the alarm clock for 3.00 a.m., my hands trembling.

Events of the First Week

My first week taught me a great deal about the activity of the fish on the Lake. I discovered that the dead period was between 1.00 p.m. and 8.00 p.m., very much in accordance with tench and similar lakes in the area. This was especially so in warmer weather. Nothing moved. In fact the big fish, particularly, went pretty

My world turned upside down . . .

. . . and still they melted from me.

well invisible. An odd one might splash out in irritation perhaps but even this was a rare event. For long periods nothing disturbed a glassy surface polished by the heat and the debris of the day.

The Lake's carp population also amply demonstrated the 'vanishing syndrome'. Carp, on lightly fished lakes, have an uncanny ability to detect a human presence. No matter how quiet and unobtrusive I was being, they would hide from me – in weed, behind islands, or simply, it seems, wishing themselves away into the crystal water. When they did move it was very often at extreme range, hugging the margins. By the third day of my visit, I realised that I was, in fact, chasing them around the lake. There was a continual drift of carp away from me as I tried to get close enough to put floaters or baits to them. To catch a fish seemed impossible, and even to glimpse one was something of a feat.

If hunting did not work then I was prepared to try an ambush. I arrived on a misty dawn when nothing seemed to be moving. I settled in the south-east corner of the lake where I was canopied and utterly hidden by rhododendron bushes. I felt sure particles would be the bait here, so I put two pints of hemp and maggots spread thickly by catapult. I settled myself behind a tree three yards from the water's edge, and listened out for the Optonics and to the world coming alive. The cattle coughed constantly in the meadow across the Lake as the vapours rose from the pastures. The clock tower chimed as the quarter hours passed, and the light intensified. An enormous fish crashed out and as the sun at last appeared the rhino backs of carp moved far out from me. I realised it was their activity that was causing the waves, for there was no wind and without them the lake would have been quite still. An adder slid past me to its daytime lair under a rotten tree, an estate worker came down to sweep out the boathouse for some romantic summer-time party. The carp disappeared. Another day had begun, and my ambush had just failed.

The concept of ambush, however, still appealed to me, especially as many of the fish seemed to move frequently on the far, very heavily wooded bank. I doubt if anyone had fished that impenetrable jungle area for years, and my mind was made up to try it as soon as possible. Indeed, that very afternoon as the wind rose and pushed along that bank I decided to make the attempt and install my gear there. Two and a half, no, more like three hours, it took me to move the tackle a hundred or so yards. For much of the time I was crawling or climbing or being nettled, stung or bitten, but at last I was there in a swim unfished for many years. I bedded myself in there as though in a base camp for a mountain assault. The rest of the day was uneventful, and rain began to fall towards evening. The

Ambush laid.

night remained dead despite a heavy closeness and occasional showers.

The wet dawn soon became torrential. Between 7.00 a.m. and 10.00 a.m. the rain literally hammered down. Between 11.00 a.m. and midday it eased, but still with frequent showers that thrashed against the brolly. There was little sign of life until three fish came into the gap between island and bank and went down there. At 12.46 p.m. exactly I had my first run of this visit. The carp was initially shocked, numbed, and wandered off into the open lake. Panic at once overtook it and it doubled back and hammered into the uncharted water behind the island. I had to follow, over my boots, up to my waist. I lost the fish round a fallen pine after ten minutes. I went to the car to dry off and find fresh clothes, and also to recuperate and steady my shaking hands. I stayed on well into darkness but there were no more signs of any carp. I almost felt as if that one lost fish had passed on the warning to its brethren in the Lake.

The following day I was in the jungle ambush again. I had kept quiet for many hours until just after midday the enormous fish that I had seen during my reconnaissance on the Lake wandered into the swim. It hung about ten yards away from me for quite some minutes, and my impression of immensity from that first sighting was amply confirmed. Its length, its shoulders, and what I could see of its depth, had me astounded. I realised that I was looking at 'the flyer of '50'. How I wanted that fish! How I willed it to go down over my baits! I knew I could not expect things to be so simple, and eventually the goliath of a fish wandered off away into the Lake and was hidden from me.

I moved into my sixth day. Apart from the one lost fish I had experienced a real grueller. I was beginning to question my ambush technique, and thought more about actively hunting rather than passively trapping a carp. That morning I took two tours of the lake with a third rod, ready to tackle any fish that I should find feeding. Both trips were uneventful but I was not deterred.

Just after midday I took my third tour of the lake. Down in the eastern corner I found two fish in a scum patch. My stalking rod was a one-and-a-quarter-pound test curve, soft-action glass affair, with eight-pound line and a large quill float attached. The hook was hair rigged up with four grains of corn threaded upon the light line. I cast close to the fish and put a pouch full of corn round the float. I sat back well hidden to wait. Bubbles appeared here and there in the vicinity, then they centred increasingly around the float. It began to tremor. It lifted, travelled to the left and took a final slow dip to eternity.

Mayhem! A cut finger keeping the fish from the trees! Wet wellingtons, now wet to the knees, but here she comes! Up! Up! Into the net with her – a cracker!

That fish was an absolute wonder. Thirty-seven years old from an estate lake and possibly never caught before. No one knew her name, she had no previous addresses. She was not my biggest carp by some pounds but I gloried in the fact

An absolute wonder.

that she was a real one. Though she was not educated, she was not stupid as she hadn't been caught before. The reverse I felt was true. She had lived so long, with habits so well formed it was very difficult to break nature's mould. She was a fish in no way dependent on anglers for food. She was content without ever seeing the bait, and could grow large without ever having to take a risk.

Once again the float had proved invaluable to me. It allowed pin-point accuracy and gave exact knowledge of where the bait was lying. The float is the perfect hunter's weapon. There are severe limitations, of course, principally range, light values, and windy conditions, but any carp hunter must use the float whenever he can.

That was my only fish of the first week, and I felt that I had earned it. I had learned a great deal more about the Lake's population, and to leave was like being thrown out of Eden. I could not wait for the chance to return.

The Second Visit

To get back became an obsession. I sent letters. I awaited the postman each morning with a growing disappointment. I was subdued to the point of depression, with little interest in fishing anywhere else. It was for me the Boathouse Lake or nothing. I felt that only one carp water existed, and that not to fish there was like waiting for a slow death. Nobody else's achievements in those weeks meant a thing to me. I wandered in a half-dream world.

At last a lady called Maggie fixed it for me. She delivered a horse to the estate, and jogged my patron's memory. The phone rang, and, yes, I was back at the Boathouse Lake again. God bless Maggie! That night I bought champagne, and would have drunk it out of her very riding boot had she asked. Now the tentative plans I had made could become firm.

I still fancied the impenetrable wooded bank behind the island. The lost fish proved not just that they used the channel, but also that they fed there. And yet I did not want to saturate a sanctuary, clear them out of it, or even make them wary of it. I therefore decided just to fish there during what I considered to be the best hours of the twenty-four – from 5.00 a.m. until 10.00 a.m. and 6.00 p.m. until 11.00 p.m. Between 11.00 p.m. and 5.00 a.m. I decided I would sleep, between 10.00 a.m. and 6.00 p.m. I would stalk, write, and watch from the balcony of the boathouse. For bait I decided on a particle and a protein – tiger nuts and a meat-based paste.

It was Monday morning, and 5.00 a.m. I simply baited up the Island swim rather than strike pitch and risk scaring feeding fish. I moved in there totally at midday and spent that first morning stalking. It was not a good morning for the hunter – the clouds were too low and the wind was moderate down the lake giving a steady ripple. Moreover, the water had clouded in the weeks I had been away and visibility was more than halved. However, I did find two big carp, both in the upper twenties, half playing and occasionally feeding in the area of the cattle drink opposite my base camp.

They were very mobile for two hours at least, making long journeys out into deeper water, and even round an island before returning to the same tight area. Each time they re-met they carried out some elaborate manoeuvre of recognition. Each one put his head to the other's tail and swam in this way, round and round. It was a circling sixty-pound ring of carp, a ritual that I had witnessed on my first visit, and put down to post-spawning courtship and excitement. Not so now it seemed, but something rather more ingrained and habitual. Very occasionally they muddied the area of my bait, but I never felt confident of a take. And so I was proved correct. Around midday they departed for good. The lake went dead, and I went up to work on the veranda of the boathouse. Still, this trip, I had confidence in my tackle, end rig, pitch and bait, and I waited with longing for the sun to dip behind the islands. A little after 6.00 p.m. my baits went out for the evening.

Around 7.00 p.m. the lake fell very still. The wind swung, dropped and died, and yet very few fish showed. Indeed, I waited till midnight without so much as a brush of a fish against my line before turning in for the night to get some much needed sleep.

This first day, sadly, was typical of the entire week. I did not have a fish, never mind a run. Nor did I see the giant. But I worked hard and tried to be adaptable to changing circumstances. The lake had defeated me. There was hardly anything to report, though I did learn a little of the place's history. I heard a story, true or not I do not know, from an old man walking his dog in the park early one day.

'They all be rum uns, yer know. The whole lot of them is strange if ye were to ask me. All that money! All that wealth, and they still be mad as March hares! Take this un's Grandad if ye like. If ye look on that tower up there – yer – the folly like one – ye'll see a big searchlight affair. Ye'll never know what he put that on fer. To spy on the couples courting in the lanes he did! He'd climb up there at night, turn on the beam and pick 'em up at miles off. A proper owd devil's trick I'd say. And then – come ye with me now to this owd oak ower there. 'Ere – stand on the fence like. Yeh. That's it. Tap that branch there with me stick. Goo on. Well? What de'yer say to that? Don't sound like wood do it? No yer daft bastard it's not rotten . . . it's made of metal, that's what! Look ye carefully and ye'll see holes like! Yeh. Wi' me, are ye? Well, a water pipe led all the way from the house over there to this 'ere tree, and into the branch. He'd get guests like, shooting parties and so on, to stand where we are to admire the owd tree. Then he'd piss orf round the back, switch on a tap, and shower the poor bastards with freezin' water!'

Laughter slipped the man's cap from his head to reveal a balding, grimy skull. He half choked, blew his nose loudly on his hands, and wiped his fingers on greasy moleskin trousers. From a moleskin waistcoat he drew out a half-smoked cigarette, and a packet of Swan Vestas. 'Still,' he continued, 'The young 'un up there now is as good as we have ever had 'ere.'

And I agreed, only partly out of gratitude for his blessing me with the right to fish this hallowed lake. More, much more, lay behind my admiration for him. The Lord here had once written to me that the county was dying from the increasing pressure on its land, its water and its resources. Like an ancient cottage, he said the beams were simply giving way, and sagging under the weight. For that reason it seems he has resolved – and damn the cost – to keep secure his estate for as long as he can. His arable land is not doused with chemicals. His pasture is not poisoned by weed-killers. His estate workers keep their own cottages – not the weekender or holiday maker. His new pits the other side of the river are left to mature, unexploited, as wildlife havens. The Lake, thank goodness, is as it always was. The keeper, bless him, is secure for life. It's good, I believe, that every now and again, a place can be time warped and wrapped away safe and secure.

The Third Visit

A two week gap followed and I was consumed by burning impatience to return. Ten days of excellent weather had had me squirming. The days were warm, close, thundery with sun and occasional heavy showers. I knew my return would coincide with the end of the excellent weather. My only hope was that the water would be warm enough to keep the fish going a while once the weather broke.

I decided on corn as bait. I knew it had been much used in the 1970s but perhaps a lot had gone in then, and few fish had come out. And, of course, my one fish, the twenty-three pounder, had fallen to it earlier in the year. Corn is a lovely bait and it is perhaps too easy to feel it is blown before it actually is. Now I decided to put a lot in over the week, much more than in the past. Two to three stone would not frighten me, and I would just have to see how things progressed.

Dawn on 24 August. The lake was perfection. It was overlaid by heavy mist. The air was warm and there was no wind. The water was still, and clear of weed. Still I say . . . it was rocking with feeding carp! As light came I could make out eight different fish, and all of them were feeding hard. Though I had put a lot of corn out into my ambush point by the island by 9.00 a.m. I had had no twitches, and once again I began to stalk. Two fish were showing in the shallows on the bank opposite. I got round to them, crawled the last five yards and cast out float fish corn. Success was immediate and absolute. A big fish approached. It disappeared, at once the red quill tip went away. The fight was again a crazy one from a long fish, lean with no hump. Twenty-two pounds, two ounces! Already the third trip had been marvellous and I had a badly aching rod arm.

By 10.00 a.m. I was once again back in the jungle by my main baited area. I felt this was probably the right decision as the wind was up now and the fish seemed to be down. Even though I kept a regular binocular scan up and down the shallows I saw nothing to make me move. In fact, I saw no fish for the rest of the morning anywhere in the lake.

By 4.00 p.m. my worst fears were realised. Northerly winds had got up quite sharply. The temperature was right down and now I was sitting in pullover and Barbour, where ten hours ago a shirt was all I needed. There was a chop on the water and a chill in the air and it was five hours since a carp had moved. The bobbins were perfectly still. It seemed that once again I was having the worst

Already the third trip had been marvellous.

[48]

possible fortune and the cooler air stream would make the rest of the week very hard indeed.

And so it proved. Yet there were periods of immense activity. One came in what I call my Albert Buckley day. The weather was absolutely dire. There were strong northerlies which had carried rain since the later part of the night. The temperature was 14°C down on the previous week. Things were made worse by the fact that the part of the lake that is open faces north. For the rest the water is totally tree-lined. It is as though this gap allows the wind in and then does not let it go but whips it round and round like a whirlwind. At times like this – 5.30 a.m. – I feel it must be the coldest part of East Anglia. For this week I had moved my main ambush point to the deeper water by the boathouse. The channel there attracted me in this period of quickly dropping water temperatures. To be honest there was also the added advantage of my own personal comfort: the boathouse would offer me some shelter from the appalling weather conditions. I had put a lot of corn in the previous night and had fished there from arrival on the new day. I had fired another two or three pounds out and was worrying about the quantities I should put in. Was I baiting with too little or too much? The size and number of the fish in the lake could make short work of it if they wished to. To add to the problem there was also the presence of a small bream shoal made up of big fish.

With all these doubts, I sat as the day gloomily unfolded before me. Then Albert Buckley came into my head. Hadn't he fished in the gale? Hadn't his giant fallen in a wind 'strong enough to blow you out of your hat!'? And had not Buckley himself fished a lake with a boathouse very similar to the one I was now sheltering beneath?

It developed into a day of very strange lights – indeed it never really did grow light at all. The swallows that inhabited the boathouse were out over the lake all morning long, feeding hard in this perpetual half light. I frequently had reason to be grateful for the shelter of the building as the rain teemed down outside. I really was as snug as it was possible to be on such a foul day. At times during the morning I felt very lucky. Somehow I knew fish were in front of me. I felt I could not be far away from them. There was little weed on the bottom or the surface and the fishing at least was simple. For periods I was reminded very much of the Roman lakes in Cheshire, again on a summer holiday, but then as a boy rather than as a teacher. The year was 1965 – well over twenty years back! Then too it was very wet and wild. I had flake out as far as I could fling it on a Chapman Mark Four. Nothing had happened until late afternoon when a six-pound mirror pleased me until I thought my heart would burst! Past 4.00 p.m. – eleven hours without a twitch – and all I could think of was Albert Buckley, the lucky devil!

And then, suddenly, it all happened. I was taking a rest from writing, almost admiring the tenacious bad temper of the day, the rain on the water, the wind tugging at the trees. A big, black head scythed the water as I looked out from the pillars of the boathouse. A carp was porpoising over the bait. At last, I was alert, ready to catch the right-hand rod in its slow run. I missed the strike. I was puzzled, fretting. I prepared another hook bait but as I did so the left-hand rod sang out.

The fish was big, a torpedo against the pressure I put on to keep it from the boathouse stanchions and, opposite, the equally deadly sweeping alder fringe. I sobbed with relief when finally I folded it in the net. Twenty-six pounds, four ounces! I had bettered Albert Buckley by four ounces! He landed his fish some five hours earlier on the day – and some fifty-seven years earlier to boot!

My last day of this third visit is well worth recording. It was 28 August and a far better day. There was some weak sunshine, the wind had decreased and there had been no rain for perhaps a dozen or more hours. The world seemed an infinitely more friendly place. The night had been cold, however, and the wind still had its edge. I was sitting with pullover, Puffa and Barbour jacket as protection against the late summer weather!

At approximately 9.00 a.m., for my watch had failed in the face of the rain, I had a lift and then a run on my right hand rod. It was a strong fish that kept going. I put pressure on and on and the damned hook straightened and pulled. Was that the monster? The chances were perhaps eight or nine to one against. It was a race, anyway, that I was miserable to have lost.

This is the horror of big fish – this exotic mixture of beauty, loneliness, elation and despair all overlaid with hours, days even, of physical inactivity and mental activity as yet another plan is hatched. My fear was that, one fish lost, I would play the next with a more sparing hand and he would get somewhere nasty and break me. Then all my confidence would be used up and I was afraid I would then be good for nothing. On a high a man can do little wrong, on a low his spirits plummet and with them goes his efficiency.

At 6.00 p.m. I had my second run in fifteen hours. Like a fool, I carried out the feeble course of action I had already predicted for myself. The nightmare of the bent hook was in my mind and I put too little pressure on the fish. There was a grind as the carp and then the bomb reached the alder fringe and snagged there. I saw a huge tail wavering in the now fitful sunlight.

Stripping, in I went. The silt was piled three decades thick at the boathouse bank. I waded out further and now there was more water and less silt. Now I was up to my chest and soon up to my chin. Half treading water, on I went, to reach the place where I had been putting the right hand bait. The water there was very slightly shallower, but wonder of wonders, the bottom was firm sand. I felt it scrunch between my toes.

The fish on course for the alders.

I reached the alders. There had been little activity for a long while and no wonder, for the line was broken beneath the bomb. The fish of that vast tail was gone. I walked back over the sand plateau and explored it with my feet. On every side it sloped away to thick surrounding ooze. It was only a small area kept clean I guess by springs or wind movement. So, that last great fish got away and though I fished on till nightfall and beyond, I did not expect another run and not one, on my last day at the Boathouse Lake, did I get.

September Return

By September I still could not get the thought of the massive Boathouse fish out of my head. However, my six days a week school job reared its head once more and to fish merely on Sundays for such a carp I could not do. For a quest like this I never really feel a single day could give me the time to adjust to the water, to read its moods or score any really deserved victories. If I were to pursue my quest, therefore, I would have to go most days, even though the sessions would necessarily be short. I would expect to arrive at 5.00 p.m. and fish until 7.00 p.m.

or 8.00 p.m. before marking and other work forced me away. As a result any attempt at ambush had to be scrapped. It was all hunting now.

I can only compare my whole approach to the way that I like best to fly fish; to travel light, to watch for a feeding fish and to pursue that one alone with real intensity of purpose. If I did not see any carp during my two hours a day, then I reckoned it quite likely I would come away without wetting a line. To cast a bait out at random for an hour or so seemed quite pointless – especially when I had stayed so long in the past and failed in the best prepared of pitches.

Like a fly angler, I felt it best to fish as light as possible. A single rod, a net, a Barbour with pockets full of bits and pieces, a box of bait and that would be all. I would not even take a rod rest which in itself is a bonus . . . putting a rest into any type of bank disturbs carp as much as anything, I believe.

I am never happier carp fishing than with a float. The float is made for the stalking approach. Every twist and turn of the game is monitored. When hunting carp in this way there is no alternative to float fishing for me – but which float? For a long while I have stuck to my quills, which I still use in flat or near calms. Come autumn though, there is nearly always a sneaky breeze somewhere and I have moved on to a Drennan Mini Drift Beater to combat this. A size six backstop, two feet up the line from the float, makes a whole rig rock solid, even in a strong push of wind over shallow water.

Baits for the hunting approach must, in my belief, be particles. Sifting through every possible particle, I decided to settle happily on maggot. There are very few carp who do not love them. At the Boathouse Lake they have not been tried for years and the nuisance fish were few. Also, now in the autumn, I made quite sure I never travelled without lobworms. Quite why lobs have dropped out of the carping scene I do not know, unless it is laziness and a slavish following of fashion. As a natural bait for the stalker, a lob is supreme and I was quite hopeful of tempting any carp on the shallows that should see one.

I look on those early evenings at the Boathouse Lake as some of my most cherished sessions there. Each day at school passed so quickly with the prospect of excitement, challenge and seclusion to come. The weather too, was at its best with frequent blue skies and awe inspiring Norfolk sunsets. The evenings were invariably warm and the leaves of the woodlands gradually turned from true green to deeper yellows and golds as the weeks progressed. The very walk to the water was always a joy to me after the city, through the copses bursting with late summer life, with the anger of jays and the alarm of pheasants. Every approach I made was literally on tiptoes. I wanted my presence to be absolutely undetected. I wanted my arrival to be unremarked by all. I wanted to drift into the life of the waterside as naturally as a passing cloud. As I crept through the last of the saplings and took out my binoculars, I could tell if I had been successful. Was a

Travelling light.

dabchick still on her old, spring nest? Was the fox still on his sandy earth on the western bank? Was there a carp basking perhaps on the scum line ten yards from the shore? If so, all was well, my presence had been accepted, absorbed into the evening like a leaf on to the earth and I could fish in perfect confidence.

For a short two hours it is possible to concentrate at a very high level and I felt an awareness of everything happening around me and in the water. The sessions passed magically quickly even though, as I had expected, most times I had not even put a bait out. That first week all I really did was establish which fish were moving where and how best I could put bait to them when a good opportunity arose. I did not see the largest fish in the lake. However one fish in particular caught my attention, easily recognisable as he was by a row of bright, brassy scales down his back. Evening after evening he cruised the top shallows before working in the bank. He travelled very slowly, occasionally rolling, even more occasionally disturbing one or two huge mushrooms of silt. Of course, as was usual at the Boathouse Lake, he refused all types of floater and for some days ignored maggots and the occasional worm cast well ahead of him as well. My fascination in him grew. He seemed the biggest of the handful of fish that were moving regularly each evening. I was fast revering his caution, but the predictability of his route made him vulnerable.

There was very little back cover, either up by the island or down the north bank and I felt pretty sure the fish sensed my presence. At the very end of his beat, however, where the water deepened two to three feet, an isolated willow grew out. On something like the eleventh or twelfth evening I got behind this, snuggled well down and plastered the drop off with one pint of maggot. At 6.30 p.m. I did not need binoculars to see the fish at the top of the bank swimming towards me. No, he head and shouldered well clear and the sun caught him in a scimitar of gold. It was 7.10 p.m. when he reached me and passed over the maggots. He circled twice and then dropped over them, feeding hard. I watched him for ten minutes until satisfied that he was well engrossed and then picked up the rod. Before I had even baited though, he was away and hidden in deeper water. My chance that evening was gone but the way forward seemed clear.

The next day's school raced by. In the late afternoon I hurtled up the river valley. Damn! There were men fishing on the north bank. They were staying on the estate and sat there like proverbial sore thumbs for three days, their lines strung out like cheese wire. Not a fish so much as fanned the boilies they had put out. Even after the last of their cartload of gear had gone, it took forty-eight hours for the lake to settle down and for the carp to re-emerge.

It was, I guess, the seventeenth night before the carp I called Brassy Scales felt sufficiently secure to resume his former life style and appear at sundown up by the island. Again I fed him maggots off the willow tree and again he fed avidly for ten minutes before the anonymity of deeper water and drawing darkness pulled him away.

And so, on that eighteenth evening, I was well ready. If he was only going to feed for a short while, I decided to reduce the number of maggots and so, at 5.45 p.m. I catapulted out a mere quarter of a pint. My own bait followed them – a bunch of three on a size 12. The red wind beater settled nicely, the line was well sunk, and the rod laid with care against a snag-free willow stump. I lay back, binoculars trained up the bank to my right.

Brassy Scales was early. A little after 6.00 p.m. he was cruising the bank and at 6.15 p.m. – a whole hour early – he was over the maggots. He browsed for only a minute and left, leaving me deflated! Twenty minutes passed. Should I leave? Should I look elsewhere? Stay I did and glad I was for just before 7.00 p.m. bubbles appeared on the fringe of deeper water. Through binoculars I could just see a large shape well down. I concentrated on the float and now there were bubbles even closer to it. A meandering chain led to the tip of red and, as if in a textbook, it dipped and slid away. The bottom of silt rocketed to the strike and the carbon hoop to the storm. For that moment in life when it seems that perfection is achieved, it is like finding the combination to a safe and the door is opened on to unbelievable treasures. That was how I felt, when in the warm

Delight in a successful campaign.

light, Brassy Scales at last succumbed and sank into the meshes of the net held out for him. I had read the water, I had chosen my fish, I planned for him and in the end everything had come together in the shape of this lovely carp throwing cascades of water at the setting sun.

The fish was not quite thirty pounds, not that I cared. Three pounds or thirty, my pleasure in it would have been much the same. For again, just like fly fishing, it is not the fish that counts always, so much as the way of the catching. I laid the fish on wet sacking and removed the hook. I remembered how, as a boy in the North, a test of a good roach or gudgeon was if it exceeded the length of the float it had just dragged under. I noticed the wind beater was just about as long as this carp's pectoral fin and I chuckled and went home from the Boathouse Lake once more a very happy man.

Winter and the Two Twenties

All through the autumn the thought of that one huge fish that had eluded me grew and grew. That was why, on 28 December 1987 I was back on the Lake after this one carp. Always before, I had believed that each fish most probably has its own season; that carp and tench belong to the summer, just as roach do to the autumn and spring and pike to the winter. Though I knew carp could be caught in the cold months and I had done so myself, I had never seriously considered them a prime objective. There was simply too much other exciting fishing to be done. But, this Boathouse Lake carp was different. During October and November my memories of its size grew. I remembered it on occasional lazy days of the summer when it hung massively on the surface of the Lake, nearly always far out, rolling, porpoising, drifting amidst the scum and flotsam of July breezes. My fear also was constant. That he was one of the two heartbreak losses on my last day of the summer. I was terrified a hard winter could kill off these vulnerable old fish. Permission to fish this most private of lakes could always be denied me. So, piece by piece the inevitability of a Christmas campaign built up inside me and a letter was written. I was in! I was back on the Boathouse Lake for late December.

I began to prebait over four weeks before the eventual day. I chose the main summer swim in the north-east corner of the Lake. Deeper water and facing the prevailing winds, plus the older screening and the shelter of the boathouse for my own personal comfort, combined to make it seem the obvious choice. I did not bait up every day – once or twice hard frosts put a skim of ice over to defeat me – but amounts gradually built up. My desire was to keep fish on the move, looking for food, in some state of awareness and not to let them slip into any form of comatose lethargy. Christmas week arrived, the weather grew very mild and I had some proof carp were moving. On two occasions fish rolled and once a carp bow waved at a careless approach to the water. So, there was at least life down there in the water that was slightly cloudier than during the summer. My dreams, I felt, were flickering towards some reality.

On 28 December the wind was fresh from the south-west and the night temperatures had only fallen to 6°C. During the day it was forecast to rise as high as 13°C. I could not wish for more perfect weather for the start of the campaign. Bluebottles came from the cracks in the wood and brickwork of the boathouse around me. There were occasional flies on the water and even Daphnia and water boatmen around the margins. Only an hour before dark, when two herons came into the island roost, did my breath condense. It was more like some of my days in summer. The morning was quiet. There was not a bleep from the indicators and not a sighting on the water. But as the wind died, around 3.30 p.m., a fish leapt in the swim and ten minutes later a run registered on the right hand rod. Even as I was playing that, the left hand rod was also streaming line out. I landed the first fish – twenty-two and a half pounds. I turned immediately to the other rod still vibrating. Twenty-one pounds! I had wanted, for a long time, my first winter twenty and now I had taken two in something under ten minutes! Both were exceptional fish, very hard fighting and very much deeper brown than in the summer. When I looked at the dark

Two winter 20lb mirrors.

mahogany of the first fish I felt it was some type of fluke. The second fish, however, was exactly the same shade. The day had been magnificent... magnificent.

On 29 December temperatures were again a blissfully mild 13°C and the sky was overcast with occasional drizzle. There was a strong ripple on the water which I liked. I began fishing at dawn once more and the light was very slow in coming, making a short day even shorter. There would be only seven hours of real daylight to be expected. I used my binoculars constantly to watch for traces – for bubbles, for a fin or for a flat on the ripple. All morning, however, the lake was dead. Midday and literally rod out, a great brown leather lifted itself out, hanging on the wind and its pectorals for a second before wallowing back through the vortex of swirling brown leaves. It was a marvellous 'hello' from a fish that looked to be well over the twenty pound mark. Later in the day, at around 2.00 p.m. I saw it cruise right, left, just subsurface in the swim. After it had gone through, I put a handful of bait along its route and plopped a rod out. It sat there untouched until after dark. At four o'clock I had a line bite on the left rod. At 4.20 p.m., a line bite came on the right rod. At 4.50 p.m. a screaming run came once more to the right hand rod. I grabbed at the handle and pulled the rod back. There was nothing. Puzzled in the extreme and disappointed, I packed and left for the day.

On 30 December it was mild and overcast but now with a thinner cloud cover. The wind too had died to make the water perfect for spotting. The bream shoal showed around 10.00 a.m. but apart from that everything was quiet and later a slightly rising wind made observation impossible. All the while I was expecting carp. There were occasional bleeps as, between me and the bait, unseen fish brushed the line. The morning wore on. I was totally alone and the lake seemed perfection and serenity. A far off chain-saw was the only sound apart from the occasional tractor somewhere on the estate. The fascination of winter carping struck me for the first time that morning. I was privileged to be alone on this crowded planet, but even more than that was the mystery of the lake before me. Chris Yates has described the power of carp fishing as long periods of inactivity, punctuated by short periods of frantic activity. This seems enhanced in the winter. There are hardly any clues offered by the steamy water. There are no carp cruising, rolling or bubbling. The water is secretive and offers no suggestions and no guidance. The wait seems interminable when out of the thin winter skies, the buzzer sounds. It seems the purest magic in certain ways.

There was still nothing by 3.00 p.m. and the rain began, the steady heavy rain that made me glad of the shelter of the boathouse. I left at about 6.00 p.m. It had been a dead day in every single way but I still could not wait for the next morning. Then, the overnight rain had cleared and it was still mild but with more wind to push the water around. Despite this I was in for another very slow day. In fact my only fun was trying to photograph a winter bat at twilight. The results, I had no doubt, would be disastrous. Yet, I stayed late, until 8.00 p.m. As I left I saw that the Hall was brilliantly lit and a procession of cars was streaming to the estate's festivities. I contrasted the secrecy of the inky carp pool at the bottom of the pasture to the splendour of the hall of light above me, and left a quiet, happy man.

The New Year dawned. I was back way before dawn and the Hall was quiet now. The whole world was utterly still but for the pines swinging in the constant south-westerly winds. Darkness was only just breaking when I had a fast run and experienced a fight that absolutely took my breath away. There was nothing I could do with this fish for over half an hour. He seemed determined to wreck me and to wreck my tackle in frantic bids to escape. At times I felt my wrist would crack to keep him from the older fringe to my right, but at last he hit the net. And what a fish! My best ever leather – twenty-five and a quarter pounds of deep chestnut brown. How the colours of these marvellous fish enrich themselves and intensify in the winter. This was like a bullet of the most solid mahogany. It was a quite superb start to my New Year. The rest of the day was very quiet. I hate drawing conclusions about fishing but I was beginning to believe the fish to be moving only very slowly. They were certainly not comatose but the summer

A bullet of solid mahogany.

pace was well reduced. They had displayed a liking for darkness feeding and my most obvious plan was to stay out all night and scrap the day. I could arrive at 4.00 p.m. and fish through till 7.00 a.m. or 8.00 a.m. This would make a fifteen hour or more vigil. Bivvying was not allowed – it is not my style anyway – but the nights were warm and the thought of the monster was ever in my mind.

The monsters of the carp world . . . just why are they so enigmatic? One thinks of the Redmire monsters and half wonders if they or my Boathouse Lake monsters ever really exist now or did so. Did I see something in the Boathouse Lake or did I see what I wanted to see? I knew to my own satisfaction what I saw, but proof is something else. I am sure Hutchinson, Yatesy, Price, Walker and all the rest at Redmire felt the same, but why the monsters do not fall defies logic. They are the biggest fish and should need that much more to eat and should, therefore, be the easiest or the first to be caught. But it never appears to be so.

It is almost as though the monsters exist on their own plane. They are fish outside normal carping techniques and knowledge. There have probably only been a dozen or so such fish ever in the country – or a dozen or so such fantasies.

On 2 January a combination of circumstances denied me fishing in the morning. On the spur of the moment I decided on an all nighter. I soon wished that I had attempted this earlier in my week for it was a night of voracious winds.

They were so strong, in fact, that a small tree came down in the park close by and the boathouse itself seemed in danger of collapse. There was no chance of sleep for me, and I was in some fear of the flying debris. The drift on the water was enormous, and the bobbins had to be reweighted. Broken branches were a constant menace, and I was glad to get out shortly after midnight, especially as another wild sleet storm was bouncing down around me.

The next day was my last. Again there were strong winds. It was bright in the morning, but steadily clouded over as the day progressed. The weather was far colder than for days. There was little for me to do but keep warm, looking out over the lake, savouring its atmosphere and locking it away in my heart for ever. There were sweeping violet clouds over the Hall in the late afternoon and they brought with them occasional curtains of sleet. Gulls, in from the coast, wheeled in the last of the light. There were no bats working on this my last afternoon and the carp remained dour until I packed and finally left once and for all.

Second Summer

My success in the autumn with Brassy Scales appealed to me. Increasingly it seemed that in order to put the largest fish from the Boathouse Lake into my net and on the bank some type of selective fishing would be necessary. Increasingly my thoughts turned once more to fishing on the top.

On my first trip of the new summer a great many fish were in the shallows at the top of the lake, basking in the warm sunlight. For the whole day they were there cruising in and out of weed beds generally relaxing and seemingly enjoying the day. For eight hours I put a succession of different floating baits over them. Every conceivable variety, shape, colour and scent was fed into them in the most seductive of fashions. The carp were clearly not afraid of the baits on the surface but not once did a single fish even move close to investigate. I might just as well have been throwing in pieces of cardboard. The day, therefore, was massively frustrating but saved by one particular fish. It swam with Brassy Scales for quite some while and I was able to get a very exact impression of its size. I do not believe it was the monster that I had seen the previous year. However, it was certainly six or seven pounds larger than Brassy Scales. It was a magnificent fish, and one I was quite desperate to catch somehow or another.

I went home very confused over the reaction of the fish to my floating armoury. I had failed to get them up before in the past and so I was not totally surprised. Thinking it over back in my study, I remembered that Tim Paisley had opinions on rich waters and floating baits. I wrote to him at once asking his

The big fish that swam with Brassy Scales.

advice. Surely, I said, the lake was a perfect float of water – shallow, clear, sheltered and quick to warm. Tim, bless him, was quick to reply.

Now you ask about the failure of surface baits. I feel it is something to do with the pH at the surface of certain waters. I am almost certain, no – I know, that smell is the passage of the hydrogen ion; pH is a measure of hydrogen ions in the water, with pH7 as neutral. I think that the further you move away from the neutral the more confused underwater smell becomes. As you move into acidity or alkalinity, the balance of the hydrogen ions becomes distorted, which I think causes a sort of ionic turbulence – for want of a better expression. The pH of the water is not an overall constant. It tends to be layerised. A water of high pH will tend to be extremely high in the surface layers, which means that the ionic turbulence will distort, or even negate, smell at that level. In other words, the smell factor, the hydrogen ion, will not pass from food source to receptor. Carp feed by smell, so if they can't smell something they will not recognise it as food. A food they will accept on the bottom may be ignored at the surface. All of this is theory, but it is the only theory that makes sense of a readily observable phenomenon. In my experience, the waters where carp do not take off the top are all waters of high pH. The best surface feeding waters tend to be acidic ones, where recognition can be a bit hit and miss on the bottom. You have made me think now. I have fished one of these waters and it could just be that boosting the natural attractors could overcome this turbulence factor. I'll try it!

Kindest regards, Tim.

My reply to Tim was vastly long and covered most of the events of that summer week at the Boathouse Lake. As a result Tim has allowed me to include this in the book.

Dear Tim,

Many thanks for the letter – all of which I found fascinating. The biologist in question also said that what you wrote made perfect and fascinating sense which I knew it would of course. The water I am discussing is very rich indeed with a very high pH value if my pieces of litmus-paper are to be believed and so that side at least fits entirely into your thesis. Certainly, too, the carp do not appear to be frightened of floating bait. They will waddle past it and even collect it on their backs. It is just that they do not seem to recognise it as food – exactly as you suggest might be the case.

The water was last seriously fished in the 1970s and I had half believed that the fish, which are the same as then, had been caught off the top and learnt a lesson never to be forgotten. Now, I think that idea is really straining credibility to breaking-point! It occurs to me that Redmire is not a totally different water – a rich estate lake with a stock of big, old carp. There too, from what I have read, they are reluctant to surface feed. I remember Ritchie 'Mac' telling me how he *covered* the surface of Redmire with floaters and did not get a single fish up. I and the angling world will hang upon words of your future experiments with more concentrated smells.

A lot of my late reply is to do with a recent trip to the Boathouse Lake, followed by a three week stint after ferox in Scotland. Your new book arrived just before the Boathouse Lake session and I took it with me to read in the periods – long ones – of inactivity of eight days and nights. In short, I think it is really, really good and there were elements that helped whilst I was there. Take your chapter "The Session". Can I quote you? You say how you were pleased with the way you were coping mentally with a long time at the waterside. At first, I felt that a little over the top. Fishing is *fun*. Or is it? It should be! Now, I adore the Boathouse Lake, but things started to go wrong there.

Rarely had I seen people on the water before but when I arrived I found builders working on the old boathouse. The aura of the place wobbled and was totally, I felt, destroyed when some anglers staying in a holiday cottage arrived to fish during my week. I decided to fish at night to avoid both pests. No use! Tuesday night I arrived and I was horrified to see the holiday men still there – on the high bank exposed to all the lake. Their cars were with them; their wives; picnic gear; I sat head in hands! In high dudgeon and with total professionalism I set up as far off as possible and settled down in mental torment to face the dusk. At 9 o'clock a big fish leapt in the mid lake. It carried on leaping. There were shouts from the bank. Oh no! They were in! They, the absolute no hopers, were into a fish. I sat in utter despair. Everything was silhouetted in the sunset.

And then something different took over. There were half a dozen different voices of congratulation and wonderment. "It's massive," "Robbie, well, well done," a voice trembled with emotion. "Twenty-six. My best. My best yet." "Put the girl back. Don't hurt her." "Rob, well done old son!" "No, I won't come back yet, I'll sit here awhile. Tell her if you see her when you go up. I'll be along sometime." "Right Robbo just enjoy it. Drink it in while you can." "The whole week's been worthwhile now." "The week, mate, the bloody season I'd say!"

A little later the car drove hurriedly over the meadow. A woman – wife, girlfriend, whatever – ran over the grass. Robbo met her halfway. They embraced

A very professional approach.

for a couple of minutes there in the dusk. She left again. I felt frankly ashamed. Carp are the fish of every deserving man. The night seemed better for all that though it became fearfully cold and I felt there was little chance of a fish. A fretful doze was all I could manage – easily disturbed by a ferocious snorting from my pitch. Silhouetted against the starbright water was a dark shape: a hedgehog feeding on spilled bait. By dawn we were getting quite friendly enough for him to take seeds from my fingers. He reminded me of a little vole years ago on the Wensum when doe bobbins in the torch beam were our only indication. One day this constant friend had four arms hooked over the line and was nibbling on the bobbin itself. I had a bite. The vole was still there at the rod butt. So was the roach. Neither would let go of the bread at either end! So, perhaps, yes. By the end of that night I was coping better mentally with my carp fishing than I had been at the start. Thanks, Tim, for that.

I also agree totally with what you say about hot spots or in your words "localised feeding spots". I have found at the Boathouse Lake that though the carp may be mobile, they only actually feed in the smallest of areas. Here, it is nothing to do with angling pressure, but only with natural phenomena. I believe that for some reason particular areas of the bottom hold some attraction for them. Perhaps winds or springs clear an area of silt and bottom weed and the carp start to browse there. Once feeding has started in earnest, then habit tends to take over and they tip up to inspect the area at every passover. This action causes a slight indentation, which in itself catches food and the circle is thus intensified.

I do not think these hot spots remain constant, but can change over a season for a variety of reasons. Indeed, if just one carp begins to browse in a small area, he clears it of weed and silt and it becomes attractive to more than him alone. I am very fortunate that there is a balcony giving me height to observe this type of behaviour, which, here, is not rare at all. It is similar, I believe, to a hot spot on the Wensum where a brick created turbulence and caught passing food. The barbel stopped there to look for food and the depression grew. Food supplies increased there even more as a result and a feeding pattern was created.

Obviously I was fascinated by what you said on carp fishing methods for I do believe that no one in the carp world knows more about them than you. The chapter called "The Channel" I found inspiring as a story but also I loved the philosophy behind it in the first few lines – can I quote you? "The modern carp fishing method is effective, the bare hook rigs and heavy bombs are designed to make the fish run. It is worth remembering that it isn't always wise to make them run, particularly when you are fishing near or against heavy snags.

We used to be far more inventive about our carp fishing before the rigs became available. In the 1970s and at the beginning of the 1980s, I caught a great many carp by actually fishing for them – float fishing, link ledger fishing, twitcher hitting on link ledgers and fixed paternosters. I think that some of the current carp anglers are perhaps growing up with the impression that you can catch a carp only

Observations from the balcony.

by making it run. That is far from being the case."

Tim, I think this is very true. During my week there was a particular fish I was very keen to catch. He was a large beautifully coloured mirror somewhere in the mid to upper thirties – you can imagine my excitement with him! My true desire was to hunt that fish. I wanted to stalk him, find him, make him feed, put a bait on him and catch him. However the vile weather of my days there prevented such observation. All I could find out was that he frequented the back of an island and appeared there most mornings between 6.00 a.m. and 8.00 a.m. As a result I adopted the traditional carp fishing method. I laid an ambush of baits, sat behind normal terminal gear and waited for the Optonics to tell me of success. I was a trapper in the best modern carp style.

My fishing bank is very overgrown with the open lake to my right. Straight out and to the left – at about twenty yards range – is a snag ridden island, the patrol path of this big fish. Sometimes it would cruise three or four yards from the island but mostly far closer. Other fish did use the area but he, my target fish, rode higher. Or perhaps it was just because he had a steeper, bigger back! I put bait on the point of the island straight in front of me, hoping to entice him out of cover.

Three days passed uneventfully before 9.00 a.m. on the fourth day saw him coming rather later than usual. There was a bow wave and a back five, perhaps six inches proud of the surface. He got to the point of the island where the bait was and disappeared in a steady swirl. Forty-five seconds later the left hand rod was screaming out and I knew exactly who was responsible. For two minutes I guess – it seemed like five – he thrashed to get to the island. It was classic stuff. There was

Dawn.

[65]

Bailey – hardly being inventive!

The carp run.

Bringing him in.

Netted!

Bailey's smallest mirror yet from the Lake.

foam everywhere and the rhododendron branches were shaking. I had to hang on. I turned him and he headed across my right into the main body of the lake. I breathed again. There the battle continued with strong runs of seventy to eighty yards but ever more into open water and I didn't care a jot about that. Eventually even this beast's heart began to falter a little. Soon he was wallowing five yards in front of me. His length, depth, girth, everything was apparent, even his eyes, his scales, his very barbules. He was mine, I knew it. I stooped for the net. Perhaps I gave him a second of slack or changed the angle of the line but whatever, the hook hold was gone. The carp righted and plunged away free, across the water.

It was minutes before I could even reel in. When I did my hook was over half straightened out – presumably holding the carp from the island. It's grim to lose a whacker, eh! And you think what has it all been for. You've broken your own spirit, wrecked your whole outlook and even life for days and caused a splendid creature incalculable distress. I hate it. I always feel that if I am going to upset a fish at least I can jolly well land it and show some purpose. I suppose that is why I liked roach fishing for so long – they don't fight back!

The modern carp fishing method was perhaps a stupid one to use there. By making that fish bolt I was forced into hanging on and holding him hard. Had I used my normal beloved float I would have had a few seconds of calm in which to steer him away from potential disaster. As it was I had a tiger by the tail, an alarmed one, one dashing pell-mell for sanctuary before I knew anything much about it. I cannot blame my gear. The rod, line and hook were all the right ones. No, I must put the loss of this big fish down to my laziness and misuse of the carp fishing method.

As you will have gathered, I am enthralled with the Boathouse Lake and I do apologise for mentioning the size and numbers of the fish that I have had there. Honestly, it is not the statistics that make me love the water but the beauty of it. It has a serenity that I associated with carp fishing when I started in the early 1960s. Nor is it all romance. Like all estate lakes now it is gin clear and a massive amount can be learnt. Carp are your thing primarily, but this crystal water does show all species up to be very bright indeed.

An adjoining lake holds some big tench. Now last year, they would not pick up a hooked bait off the bottom: it was just too heavy for the gentle suck they were giving it. A polystyrene insert was needed to lift the bait more easily into the mouth and Miller and I were the only ones catching again.

This season, first day, we were in the same swim and in the same gear, all ready to go. Sure enough, at first light a big tench comes along, head down, feeding hard on the baits. He gets to within two feet of my float, a small crystal and he stops, levels out and bolts off into the blue beyond. Now that tench had not seen terminal tackle for close on a year but he remembered and for us it was back to the drawing-board. Like you, I was brought up with the harder-fished waters of the

Tench in profile.

Miller catching again.

North, but that does not mean these "wild" fish are easy. Their comparative lack of sophistication brings its own problems.

I will attend to the matter of the chapter. You have every right to call in a marker. I owe you a hell of a lot!

Best fishes, John.

3

The Wye

It is easily possible to love rivers, just as easily in fact as human beings themselves. Both have beauty, character, and both have good and bad moods. You can feel at ease in the company of a river. They can soothe like a mother, interest like a teacher or even excite at times like a lover. Rivers roll on through history and make their own marvellous legends. They give off a charisma. They can, simply, be magic. So it is anyway with the mighty Wye. The very first time I saw her, I was smitten. Her body overwhelmed me – wide, deep, then shallow; pools, bends, still eddies, rapids, islands. Clear at times, murky at others. Tree-lined everywhere with willows, alders and oaks. Her landscape is also important. The Wye has wide floodplains, all heavy with cattle. There is a constant sense of hills on the horizon. You feel they are soft and easy and yet

Beauty and character – the Wye.

somehow they are grand and mysterious at the same time. The Wye is a river of superb dawns and romantic dusks. It is dotted with villages, half Welsh and half English, where cottages are still predominant. Even the towns along the Wye are still recognisable as ancient gatherings. Ross is resplendent on its cliffs and Hay is an ancient town of narrow, steep streets dotted with bookshops and street cafes. It has a sense of openness, of generosity and is a happy place, cheerful even in rain. Above all the Wye holds the most fantastic fish stocks. One place in particular will ever be in my memory. I am thinking of the famous 'Uncle Sid's'.

Uncle Sid's

Chris Yates bears a great deal of responsibility for this next section for it was he who told me about Uncle Sid's in the first instance. We had met for a day's fishing on the Royalty at Christchurch. It was evening and we were sitting together by the famous Parlour. It was one of the few times I had been to the Royalty and I found the night bizarre. The river itself is so lush and natural but the town somehow so obtrusive. We were eating fish and chips by streetlight as Chris packed away his canes and his pins and all manner of secret baits into secretive little boxes. We talked about the Wye – another shared passion – and Chris told me about Uncle Sid's. He made it sound marvellous as only Chris can. I was there five weeks later and it was marvellous. Imagine...

An old house is walled off from the world. It is dawn so it is a sleeping house with the mist still hanging round its windows and gables. An equally ancient black dog is asleep in a kennel, so comfortable he merely cocks an eye, pretends to growl and sinks back into cat-catching dreams. A gate opens before you. A vegetable garden now stone-walled, peas in rows, sweetpeas in columns, lettuces crisp and green, and orderly rows of potatoes. There is a fire still smoking from yesterday's rubbish clearance and rabbits bobtailing through the chinks in the wall. Now you are at a wicket gate. There is damp cow parsley and loosestrife smelling heavy and sweet in the dew, shedding their moisture on to your trousers.

Ten more yards and there, the Wye – half awake – is before you, her breathing misting the entire valley. A lazy chub rises to a moth. There is a heavy crash of salmon making a move before full daylight. There is a heron on the shallows with a gut full of minnows. All this is a cliff face beneath you. Here the Wye runs like the Limpopo – a great green and greasy river. She is twelve feet deep and more, but depth does not hide the big chub beneath. See that one with jaws like a white whale. I know there is a great pike or two down there but Uncle Sid's shallows are where it all really happens. The walk is four hundred

The gravels at Uncle Sid's.

yards and the path follows a long-disused railway. Only badgers tunnel the place now and snort to scare you when you return at dusk.

Now, in the still air, you can hear the river. She has quickened her pace. She is diving down. We are here at Uncle Sid's rapids. They are two or three hundred yards long and the river has widened, carving islands and gullies between the bright cliff faces. The water is fast, the bed is of gravel stone and thick streamer weed. From here she empties out into a long fast glide where the grilse love to lie under a canopy of great oaks. Then the Wye drifts out into a slow conformity again. There is a mile of almost canal-like water where chub and pike predominate, but it is on Uncle Sid's rapids that we focus our attention. There is not a house in view and every human sound is drowned by the water. I wrote about it all to Chris – partly to thank him, partly out of absolute excitement.

Dear Chris,
As you know I have a project in mind: to know the river Wye. Since I saw you last I have spent weeks there. I have fished, walked, drunk, talked, walked, fished, drunk and on and on and in a never ending search for fish ... and most especially barbel of the middle Wye! Success has been very limited with these – rumours of fish here and there – some big and some massive – but little concrete to report. Thank God I find – I believe we both do – the Wye Valley one of the most stimulating places to be in this country. The mystery of the river is immense. Take

away the salmon men and the middle river is hardly fished at all. Catch a barbel –
any fish come to that – and you know it is well and truly yours and not one that
the specimen hunting world and its mother have seen over and over, named and
nearly grown to despise! Why, I recently edited a 75,000 word book for the barbel
catchers: there were 250 words on the Wye! *Nobody* knows. . .

I have had some marvellous times and have actually seen barbel. I was down
with Terry Moore in May for a good long look and spent most of my time on some
gravels below Hay. You know the place – indeed you told me about it. Uncle
Sid's! Everything was there. Whilst the rest of the river ran very low and sluggish,
these rapids attracted all life to them. Everywhere there was evidence of the
winter flood. There was a tide mark on the meadow twenty odd feet above this
low spring level. There was a big tree uprooted and left above the glide to become
a sanctuary for all kinds of fish. I had great fun with the trout – not the huge two
to three pounders Terry seems to get but ten and twelve ounce fish that are as wild
and as perfectly marked as any I have ever seen. I lost a decent grilse that was
obviously living in the glide and I annoyed a very large, rather stale spring salmon
that was lying in slightly deeper water waiting for heavy rains and a push up-river
once more.

I span for the shad that had come up there to spawn. Crazy herrings that they
are, skittering here and there in excitement. Both Terry and I saw two or three
very spectacular fish indeed and presumed them to be shad. They were quite large
– about three to four pounds – but it was their colouration that was so superb. To
me, they looked a vivid turquoise along their backs and then the brightest silver
along their deep flanks. Their fins appeared the most delicate shade of red. I say we
presumed them to be shad, but we could not catch one for a close inspection and

A chub on . . .

. . . and coming close.

Held a second before return.

nothing from our combined library seemed to describe anything particularly close to what we both saw.

There were chub there of course. They had spawned thereabouts and were happily feeding and cleaning themselves. Ninety-nine per cent of them were under four and a half pounds. One fish looked seven pounds or more. I thought at first he was a common carp wandered in from a certain lake at Ross! Pike, of course, were there in numbers – shad dying all around – the chance of an unwary grilse, the possibility of a dead kelt salmon drifting past or a big red springer keeling over – all too good for a predator to miss.

Now I come to it. I saw two barbel! Lying in the turbulence of a fallen tree were two fish of, I guess, eight pounds and eleven to twelve pounds. I saw them once, clearly, for two to three minutes and from then, only in tantalising glimpses. I believe Terry was with me at least once when I saw them, but phoned later to say they had been there well on into June. A week or so ago I went back to catch them. I spent a morning looking. It was a Saturday and there was some kind of festival on in Hay up-river. I found them in early afternoon and I knew I would have to approach from the shingle bank. I settled myself down amidst reed cover. With the greatest patience I began to feed in bait. After an hour a barbel hashed. This was getting close. I began to shake a little.

Up-river there were shouts. Mighty ripples swelled past. The Hay canoe regatta – or whatever! Seventy canoes all careered to the shallows. There were fights, duckings, and an hour later they left me by a totally wrecked piece of river. The barbel did not return.

The last days of the visit were spent walking and watching on the beat I fancied the most – that controlled by the Red Lion at Bredwardine. I covered all eight miles of water and salmon fished a little to get the idea of depths, flows and bottom make up. I talked to the gillies and the locals and I *know* this is the place for big barbel. Those up at Hay are pioneers. Here, they have settled and even bred but still there is absolutely no *pressure* on them.

Salmon fishing ends on 17 October and then coarse fishing is open to those few residents who desire it. The last week of October is when I hope at last to get my Wye barbel to complete a quest that is very dear to me. The trouble is, I realise it will be hard – a lot of water, few guide marks, possibly cold weather, perhaps flood. Without company my heart could be in my boots in no time. Miller is keen to join me. We feel a third would be of great benefit, but almost the only guy we would be happy to include is you. How about it? The last week in October on the Bredwardine Wye after barbel that might not even be there. Can you make it or will Miller and I be alone before the storm? Give it some thought, Chris, please, before saying no.

I had one reply. It seemed to look good.

Dear John,
Please forgive the delay in replying to your superb letter of 21 July. I was on holiday when it arrived. (All my life is a holiday, but it's a proper holiday when we all go down to the sea with bucket and spades!) Then the Avon barbel began to move. The cold June meant they were spawning in late July and only began to get

All my life is a holiday.

into proper condition during August. So you can see that I have not been completely idle. I also spent time considering your kind request.

What you say about the Wye encapsulates precisely my own feelings towards it – and especially towards its mythical barbel. Unlike you or Terry I have never actually seen one, though I did think I had hooked one last September. I was fishing with Terry and I hooked something in a deep chub hole which did not feel like a chub. It kept low and moved slow and ponderously. I was rather out-matched with my four-pound line, light cane rod and centre pin. There were one or two tremendous upstream runs. One took over fifty yards of line and threaded it through three weed beds. Miraculously, I got it all back on the reel, and, after half an hour, Terry finally swooped with the net. I was never more disappointed to see a salmon! Ten and a half pounds! After that I was determined that one day I must catch a wild barbel.

Whenever I do a talk – which is very rare nowadays – there is always great interest when I enthuse about the Wye and its potential. But I know that no one will actually go and fish for Wye barbel, simply because, as you said, no one really knows about them. I have a Welsh spy who keeps me informed and for five years he has been telling me of any reported Wye barbel. Some have turned out to be carp but most have been authentic. After all, you cannot easily confuse a barbel with anything else. One or two specimens have turned up in matches on the Hereford stretches. A few big fish have appeared near the confluence with the Lugg. A ten pounder was landed at Monmouth but most of the barbel caught in the last seven years have come from your choice of hunting ground – the Red Lion

[77]

Terry Moore fishes at Uncle Sid's.

stretch! They have even been taken on luncheon meat there. The highest barbel I know of was caught by my good friend Bob James – the only person other than Terry who I know has caught a Wye barbel. This fish, a six pounder, was caught very high up on a lob worm.

I know very well the swim you describe below Uncle Sid's. According to Terry, the local keeper has seen barbel spawning there. I had dreams of doing what you so nearly succeeded in achieving. What an appalling anticlimax. Why should the Wye be polluted by canoeists?!

As to your grand expedition, I am certainly interested, and it is very kind of you to say that you consider me a fisherman worthy of the Wye – and your company. You must be mad! I think I could make a day or two in late October. What are your plans? Tell me more about your strategy. Will you stay at the Lion? Will you fish for the entire week? What barbel news from Bredwardine in the last twelve months? Will gaffs be compulsory? What vintage will we be drinking? Single or plaited hair? Green heart or cane? Hemp or depth charges? Tell Roger that, if I come, I don't want any of those baiting engines, adjustable rod rests or inflatable women! Perhaps it would be better for you both if I stayed on the Avon.

Bounteous barbel, Chris.

Thus assured I made plans. Rooms were booked at the Red Lion and a fourth friend, Reel Screamer, was also invited to make up the numbers. Everything boded well when I had a second letter from Chris. Note the menace of the very first line.

Dear John,

Can I attempt to modify your plans just a little. I have recently discovered, through my contacts with the Westerly lands, two shoals of big barbel up in the wilder waters of Erwood. These shoals consist not of the usual two or three fish – that's a group not a shoal – but of at least a dozen in each. What's more a tame bailiff will be happy to deposit several hundredweight of ground bait into the respective pools, just to ensure our success.

What do you think? You could still stay at the Red Lion and concentrate on their waters, coming up to Erwood for a break at the chosen time. Or, you could stay for some of the time nearer to Erwood at a friend's fishing hotel up at Builth. I know it is always a bore to disrupt a long thought out strategy but can you afford to ignore these signs?

My main contact in this matter is the eccentric doghandler and carpsnitcher Bob "Breeks" James. He is, I am afraid, only too happy to gillie for us if you choose to move up country for a day or two. He does have a superb collection of pedigree rods and reels and always wears a tie when catching big barbel so I think he might meet with your approval. He would also add to a more balanced team. Four anglers tackling two shoals will be better than three, for you would find it hard to bear if I caught all twelve from one shoal while you had to share yours. Let me know your reaction to this distraction.

Best wishes, Chris.

Wilder waters.

Wye Bother

Any angling expedition can go wrong. A lack of planning, bad information, weakness of research, poor weather – any, or all and more of these can star the quest with ill fortune. A late change of plan can also be very much for the worse. Opportunism is one thing, recklessness is entirely another and this led to one of my most foolish days ever. The plan as you have read, had been to fish the Red Lion water solely. This plan was the correct one. It was vital to stick on one stretch of the river, to build up both swims and knowledge. Then came Yates' letter with all its subtlety, guile and seduction.

I put the dilemma to Miller. Two shoals of barbel... pre-baiting... big fish... it was all more than a man can bear and so in a crisp October dawn Miller and I were speeding forty miles up the Wye Valley into darkest Wales. I was not totally happy to be leaving Bredwardine but it was bliss to be alive – then! The colours of the sky were awe inspiring, from the most brilliant of lemons in the east, to a deep blue of real promise for a fine day. The oaks that followed the road were glowing greens and golds in the frost bright light. Where we could see the great winding Wye it was steaming in the growing warmth. A little short of Builth, we were passed by Yates and Bob 'Breeks' James. We caught a glimpse of beards and deerstalkers and followed like hounds after hares. The day was on.

We reached the hotel early and had to knock up our contact there, the owner, who we shall call Jones – Alan Jones. We shook hands in the gravel courtyard. There was laughter. There was an old reminiscence to warm the cockles of friendship. We pulled on our wellingtons. We walked down a feeder to the main river to inspect the first barbel hole.

At the confluence, the chances looked superb, the water was a perfect colour and pace. There were intriguing currents, obvious holes and tantalising weed cover. 'Oh yes, yes,' Miller positively drooled. 'And how long has this been baited for us, then?' he asked. The pause was slightly long and an embarrassed Alan admitted he was not quite sure barbel were resident there. 'But they could be,' he added. 'Looking at the water, they jolly well should be!' Just a little dashed we all agreed, but quietly we were not utterly convinced.

We wandered back slowly, waiting a while at the salmon pool, where for once, a salmon failed to jump for us. Alan showed us the otter holt, too, but of course the light was too great now and the five of us had caused far too great a disturbance for the shy beast to appear.

Sad all this, but breakfast was an absolute feast in Alan's hotel. Over everything that a superb Welsh kitchen could provide, Alan introduced us to the area. The Quarry Pool sounded so mouth watering with its seven pound perch that Miller insisted on a visit there and then. Excalibur Lake, where wildies of fifteen pounds swim round the sword thrown by Arthur seemed good enough to me and I promised myself a visit the next summer. But now, we were on the tails of the barbels and we pressed Alan for the low-down.

He was, it must be said, a little disappointing, a little vague. 'But the holes?' we quizzed, 'The shoals? the pre-baiting?'

'You could try Erwood,' he said. 'Pretty well definite sightings round there, I'm told.'

'Any clues to exactly where?'

'Not really. Try the pub water. Just mention my name and they will probably put you right on it.'

We looked at the Quarry Pool and dramatic as it was, we were puzzled why the sticklebacks swam around so openly, so apparently unafraid of the striped marauders beneath them. Eventually we made it to the pub at Erwood. It had no fishing outside the salmon season. No. Nothing. We mentioned Alan's name. It unlocked no doors. Alan who? Two more pubs. Two more rejections and Yates growled, furious, 'I'll ring Jones!'

As a result, we made our way to the Bridge Inn where a man grabbed our tenner, wrote out four tickets and led us to the river before we could gulp. He pointed to a hundred yards of shallows beneath the town sewer outfall, said 'There you are, lads. Good luck', and was back in his bar as quick as an eel up a

[81]

Yates, James and Miller puzzled　　　　　　*Yates and James make a feeble attempt.*
at the Quarry Pool.

drainpipe! Miller, bless him, fished till dark for two chub. Yates spun his pin a couple of times and 'Breeks' and I just moaned.

Back at the hotel the four of us met Jones for dinner and very pleasant it was. We had been cross, but good food, wine and a crackling fire made it seem much more like fun. Relaxing now, seeing the friendship come back on to our faces, Jones told us about the carping at Llandrindod Wells – the place Yates had his first twenty pounder. God it sounded good. After all Jones had taken thirty doubles on opening night. Miller and I left in a dream for the journey back to the Red Lion at Bredwardine.

Mr James, it seems, drank overmuch that night and slept in. Yates, however, was about before dawn and spent first light and beyond hidden by the otter holt. He admitted defeat and met a startled Mrs Jones opening up the hotel. He explained what he had been doing.

'Otters?' queried Mrs Jones, 'What otters?'

The Lost Pot Fish at Bredwardine

During August 1987 I had walked the entire Bredwardine length at a time of low water. Whole areas looked immensely attractive in barbel terms but one length in particular had me riveted. The place was a named salmon pool – The Pot, I believe – where the river narrowed, deepened, quickened, and surged out in the huge rapid. This plume of fast water drove for a hundred yards or more, slamming towards a huge bend festooned with snags, overhanging alder and willows, eddies and subsidiary currents. From what I could see in the summer clear water, the bed was predominantly sand and gravel with fine weed growth. Everything seemed to scream out barbel. Though the swims were in exact midpoint between two traps in a dire walk, I was determined to fish there come the autumn.

True to my promise, late on the day of our arrival, I trekked to The Pot and introduced large quantities of luncheon meat over a fifty yard length of bank. The next morning we all three, Miller, Reel Screamer and I, made the journey and more bait went in. One large eddy in particular increasingly attracted my attention. From above the water, it seemed to have everything a barbel could need. The flow on the outside of the eddy beyond the crease was perfectly placed. The head of the eddy itself was overhung with snags and trailing branches. The bed of the eddy was gravel with fallen debris providing sanctuary

The approach to The Pot.

Reel Screamer tests the water.

The team investigates on a dull October morning.

[84]

here and there. In short, a barbel would find everything necessary for a happy life here, and I could hardly believe fish were far away.

Tuesday was wet. Before breakfast, I put more meat into my eddy, and later fished elsewhere. Early in the afternoon, I made the long walk with my tackle, hopeful that now three baitings had taken place, the barbel would be moving on to the meat with no suspicion of danger.

The light was gloomily low. Clouds of drizzle and heavier rain draped the Marcher Hills down-river, and the world around was eerily silent. But for crows on the far bank and the incessant chatter of the river, I was utterly alone. Half an hour and I was content to feed in more dribbles of meat. I took a chub of some four pounds on the first cast, at 2.30 p.m. Ten minutes rest, more meat, a second cast and a second chub. This pattern continued until 4.00 p.m. when pelting rain and a screen of cloud brought about premature darkness.

The red mud banks were awash. Pieces of meat swam like red piglets in the bait tin, and the temperatures dropped rapidly. It became a miserable session, and by 4.30 p.m. even the chub appeared to have been exhausted. On until nearly 5.00 p.m. the rod tip never wavered, and when it did at last move, I was unsure of the cause. A series of tremors attacked it – a phenomenon I put down to the slightly gusting wind, or to the river ever rising. Only when the last three feet hooped out of the torch beam, and into the night did I see the affair for real!

Immediately, I was on my feet to a power quite unlike the most sullen of chub.

Cloud-draped Marcher Hills.

The reel handle revolved round and round, quicker and quicker, then a blur, and I was stumbling along the treacherous bank, the Wye thundering at my feet. I was keeping the rod as high as possible to clear the line below the willow screen, but the pressure made it crippling on my arms, and I felt the fronds snatch as I passed. So, for fifty frightful yards I shuffled, facing death or disaster at every fearful step when – Oh no! – there was nothing but slackness on the rod, and a skimmed hook on the line. I slopped my way back to the gear, and sat shivering in the teeming rain. The Wye had risen six inches in an hour and her pace upwards was increasing, so, with no heart to try again, I packed and began the long walk back to my friends.

As I passed The Pot itself an explosion of water attracted me to the bank side. In as many minutes, three salmon belly-flopped before me in their journey upstream. Clearly the growing currents had stirred them into movement and the great fish were on the move all along the river. The obvious thought that my lost monster could well have been a salmon hit me. Of course, damn it, why hadn't I thought? Hadn't Chris Yates taken a ten pounder only a while before on meat? Now I could feel happier that, perhaps, probably even, a barbel had not been lost, but with every step gloom intermingled. Perhaps The Pot was not the place. I was probably no nearer to a barbel than before.

Probably no nearer than before.

Further Events at Bredwardine –
Chub Hole

The Wye does some remarkable things to herself: she can wriggle, stretch herself, and at Chub Hole, breathe in and nip her sides to produce a waist of extreme depth, slenderness and almost sensual laziness. Of course, she does this in private. To see her here you must walk a good two miles from the nearest track or salmon hut, and you will find the place well guarded by nettle, thorn and loosestrife. But there is no pleasure without pain, and as I picked the thorns out of me and looked down on this curvaceous piece of water, I drooled. It was next to the last day of our stay, and 11.00 a.m. I retraced my steps, met up with the other boys and we enjoyed a hearty lunch. The conversation was all Wye – or should it have been Why? Barbel now seemed a slender chance we knew – but they always had been. This energy lag had only to be expected. Miller forced himself to the Salmon Hut corner. Chris and Bob, deserting Erwood, were up-river, and a late October afternoon began to fall around us all. Low cloud and drizzle did nothing but deepen the gloom, yet it was mild. The river was fining down after the heavy rain two days before, and the Wye was preparing to show me just what she could do.

At approximately 3.30 p.m., I cast into the Hole. I counted the bomb down

A typical Wye chub.

and made it about fifteen feet in depth. I reeled in the slack, put the rod in the rest, curled the line around my finger and I was into the first chub. Like every Wye fish, he plugged away hard enough to make my heart beat, but a chub was all in truth he was, and with no pretensions grander than four pounds or so. By 5.00 p.m., I had taken fourteen chub, recording on five pounds three ounces after having slipped back a larger one unweighed. Now it was dark and the bites had changed to trembles. The meat on size sixes was scaled down a fair bit, and a one and a half pound roach came as a result. Things were now electric and in that mild, misty evening I could have expected absolutely anything, but still fallen short of reality.

On the small hook, the tip banged round. A strike. A chub? No way! This fish went – far, deep, unstoppable. I was back winding – back winding – just hanging on. A pause in mid-river – a thump – and on again upstream the battle took me. That this fish was mightily heavy I did not doubt, but it was the action that had me in prayer. Deep surges, a muscular, almost eel-like drive – I had a barbel on – surely, surely that at last!

I hollered into the night for Miller. My voice bounced fruitlessly back off the hills and drowned in the singing of the rapids. It was me and the fish, death or glory, and so for what happened you will have to believe me or not.

The rod of one and a half pounds test curve was not up to the job on hand now. I knew it. I think it did too the way it buckled under every surging run. Neither of us could do anything much with the fish. It was simply bull-like. I don't quite know how long into the fight I noticed, but I found I was trembling. The combination of damp, sweat, a sudden chilling wind, and sheer tension had me shaking in my legs, arms and all down my back. I found too that I had a blinding headache and that one wellington was awash with Wye water.

The fish was closer now, hugging the bottom beneath the rod tip. The wind was out of it all right, but the bulk weight was something to drag up that dozen resisting feet, and yet, inch by inch, I cranked the beast towards midwater. Over and over, it made a drive down again, but I held it by the horns and kept it with me. I fumbled for the big torch and spread the beam out across the Wye's black surface. The handle of the net was between my knees and I was set to finish the job at last.

Do you remember *Jaws*? – the moment when the shark was first seen close to the boat with his head scything out, great, mean and ugly? Something similar was about to be my experience now. Expecting a barbel, for a second, a chub's head and eye twinkled in the torch beam and then, in a roar of Wye, the chub rocketed upward locked in the jaws of one of the largest pike I have ever seen. The massive fish arched before me, transfixed in the light, only half a dozen feet away. It was tawny, spotted, leopard-like and it was massive.

Proof – if needed – of the size of the Wye pike.

Everything was explained – fortunately – to both man and fish! The pike spat the chub, mangled and dead, into the Wye. My spirits were just about in the same shape and if it had been day not night, the lads might just have noticed the odd tear tucked into the corner of an eye...

A Fight over the Candles

There is a manner of man in the far west of England that I as an angler had never seen the like of before. Nor had my companions who looked on him with awe similar to my own. This vision was tall, lean, heavily muscled and tattooed. He was also shaved quite bald but for a pigtail of hair in the very centre back of his head. It must be said, finally, that his eyes protruded horribly out from their sockets in the manner of a toad. As a result, even if he should ever smile, his eyes still revolved wildly and made him seem a demon. His name was Tarus Bulba and wherever he went in that valley a hush would follow him.

But we, Miller, Reel Screamer and I, had been out late on the Wye and been thoroughly soaked. The rain had carried sleet and raised the river with chilling effect. We had not caught. We had perished and we were not likely to desert a warm bar after such a night for anyone. Tarus saw our resolve. He watched us carefully over his pints. Around midnight it was deadlock: neither he nor we would wave a white flag and leave first. The poor barman sweated it out and then on the stroke of 1.00 a.m. Tarus selected Miller as the one of us to arm wrestle.

I cannot believe Miller was happy, but even when candles were placed on either side of the men's arms he did not flinch. In the lowly lit room, the contest began. Over and over did Miller's hand brush the naked flame and at last the singeing of hairs grew too strong to ignore. Tarus, seemingly satisfied, sat back. With terror in my heart, I realised I could not let my friend down.

'Take us both on, Tarus,' I said, 'if you dare.'

More candles were brought. My arm was lashed to Miller's, mine in the rear to catch the candle if the beast should ever get the better of the two of us. We began and Tarus grunted and sweated and looked woebegone, but it was my hand that began to taste the flame and it was my blood that began to boil in the vein and it was my voice that sang out 'Christ, Tarus, give us break!'

Big Reel Screamer had watched all along through drooping eyelids that now flashed with heroic dreams. He raised his mighty frame from the bench and swayed through the tables that formed the battle ring.

'Tarus', maddened, he cried, 'dare you meddle with me? ... and these two here of course.'

Our three arms were whipped as one by the leather thongs and they presented as noble a sight as any elephant's trunk. Tarus paused, drank a quart and took his seat. It was now two in the morning and we would wrestle if need be until the dawn broke over the Welsh hills. For an hour, both sides held firm, but little by little, I sensed our three strengths were gaining, inch by inch, over the giant beside us.

Sweat poured off him and glistened like the dew in the candlelight. The buttons of his horsehair shirt burst loose and the eagles on his biceps flexed their wings and began to soar ... to no avail. The eyes of Tarus started to roll in despair, like those of the whales struck through and through by hunters' harpoons. His breath came in fits and starts and his left hand sought the flagon of ale in constant desire for relief.

There was no saving him now: his great scaly hand approached the guttering flame. He pulled a knife from his sock, we looked on in terror. With a single blow he cut the leather thongs and stood up sweating profusely.

'That's enough my boys,' he said, 'well done. The next round's on me.'

It was at that moment we knew that we had an ally and friend in those Welsh borderlands.

Reflections on the Wye

Reel Screamer had gone. Chris and Bob next waved farewell. Miller and I were
soon to leave. The last night was on us and only ten fishing hours remained. It
was raining again, and the river would be rising fast. We knew pretty well that
we were done for. Had the trip failed? For barbel, yes of course, unless that lost
giant of the Pot Pool, were not, by some miracle, a salmon. But then, we had had
near on one hundred chub to over five pounds and a few hulking roach. We had
got to know the Wye far far better, and had had moments of high drama,
suspense and excitement. We had all been captivated by certain shades and lights
that had painted the valley into a fairytale. We had renewed some very warm
friendships and had had some damned good laughs – and right to the end,
navigator Miller directed me off the M5, and still at 80 m.p.h., into an Asda car
park! So if for the purist, we failed, so be it. Success all the time would soon pall.
Fishing, or life, without both ups and downs would be death. And if we had
succeeded ... why then the bar of the Red Lion would that night have runneth
over! Who knows, perhaps just one of us, one cast had a bait only inches from a
leviathan's snout? Perhaps if one of us had not reeled in that second. Or if a
different bait had been on the hook that cast...

Bait. Yes. If we were to go back to the Lion, and I hope we will, I would
change baits. Bob made this point well. In his experience of truly wild barbel,

Baiting up on the Wye – but with what?

they do take time to turn on to non-natural foods. Meat and corn are not heavily used on this salmon river and even several days of baiting might not have been enough to tempt the odd big fish into an experiment. Bob also stressed that few of us realise just how many worms find their way into a big river. He cited the fish traps on the Avon as an example. After flood or high water, he said that they groaned with drowned lobs. The Wye runs scores of miles through the richest, most fertile pasture land and that week of rain that we were on her, millions of worms must have died within her. Next time I will go with a thousand lobs and trundle them down swim after swim until I find the barbel. Then will they be able to resist my bait? I think not.

We nearly took maggots on our trip. We did not and that was a mistake. At least we would have been half way to the worm concept and they would have fared a lot better than the corn we threw in, pint after useless pint.

The lesson from Uncle Sid's also remains with me loud and clear. I cannot help remembering that I at least saw barbel there in the fast, clear water, and believe me on such a huge river, with no knowledge to guide you, location is a nightmare. Before any future trip, I would like to follow this plan: to walk as much river as possible in the late summer, whilst the salmon season is still on, but while the water is yet low and clear.

I would concentrate on the shallows and watch long for barbel activity. By baiting hard with maggots or chopped worm I might just get them flashing and

I concentrate on or near the shallows.

The Wye can produce a 40lb plus fish for the salmon man.

giving the game away. As an October return would be much more feasible, once that major nightmare of location had been partly solved, at least we could fish with confidence knowing that barbel were still in the area.

Barbel are the river carp of our country and all are wonderful creatures but a Wye fish must be special. They are still so enigmatic, one of any size must be an achievement, I, for one, would go to any lengths to secure.

The lost pike of the Chub Hole should not be ignored. With the excellent Terry Moore, I had a superb afternoon's Wye piking. On the Moccas fishery itself, I had a seventeen pounder – all muscle and dash. As I barbel fished, a pike rod and large dead bait would go with me – lowered carefully into each swim as I went. A double lob worm searching the gravels; a juicy dead bait oozing out its juices; I hardly know which I would like to go first!

Unlike some, Chris, Bob, Roger and I are sure the Wye is capable of holding the monsters we seek. One day, someone will prove us conclusively correct.

4

Ferox

Fact and Fantasy

It has become an axiom of modern coarse fishing that the pike is the ultimate predator. For most people this is so; geography dictates it. But for those willing to travel, to explore and to experiment there is a fish arguably far more charismatic than the pike. For over a century the British fisherman has known about the ferox. Few have been caught, very few are today, but their glamour remains enormous for me. Indeed some of the most tingling of angling literature concerns them, but then it is easy to write about ferox because they are unparalleled.

Men like St John and Malloch started the Victorian ferox period. Salmon, stag, grouse and ferox all dominated the late nineteenth century and Scottish hotels in the Highlands boomed as a result. Gillies became a widespread, professional class and even though the journey from the south often took two or more days, they had plenty of clients with great wealth and leisure time. Add the experience of the Scot and the passion of the English gentleman together and ferox began, from the 1850s, to be caught. It was not until the pressures on society brought about by the crises of the 1920s and 1930s that ferox slipped back into obscurity again. For half a century, avowed ferox hunters have been few.

My own obsession – for that is what it has become – with ferox, began one wet Saturday in 1962. A friend of my father's presented me with a copy of B.B.'s famous Bedside Book and all day long I sat in my bedroom, glued. Everything made an impact. This was the step out of Crabtree I needed and grasped at. I had already sampled Walker, but he did not get the blood racing in the way these stories did. And the section that had the most to offer, it seemed then, and always since, was that on ferox.

These ferox stories had the lot: a Victorian bravado and splendour; the misty appeal of gaunt Scottish lochs; the pluck and guile of long-dead gillies; battles of soul-stirring intensity and a fish held up at last as angling's ultimate prize. How I

The ferox – angling's ultimate prize.

envied MacDonald Robertson and his gillie, Nichol, as they hoisted ashore their fifteen pound Awe trout to end a story I read over and over again, just before sleep.

Of course, not yet ten then, I could do little about my passion but dream. A tench, a carp, a pike or a bream were all themselves exotic enough for my reality. Ferox, though, was a dream that did not fade with age but grew as I accumulated the resources to make an attempt. By 1974 I was ready to start northwards, with fear, longing and absolute lack of knowledge. I settled on Loch Awe in acknowledgement of glories of the past and was utterly overwhelmed there. I could not come to any terms with its size or its depths. My fishing techniques fell woefully short and I was literally dangerous in a boat on such a water.

Yet, year after year, I persevered. I never wrote a word about these exploits in the angling press for they were nothing but farce and failure. My last serious ferox shot came in 1982 when I went far north, to Sutherland and Loch Assynt. I invested a good deal of time, effort and money into that expedition, failed, and turned my back on ferox until 1987. That year, and particularly in 1988, I tried again with renewed vigour. Now I had echo sounders – an absolute essentiality. By now too, I was a better pike fisherman and more prepared for this big trout predator. I was also coming to grips with boat fishing and to be a ferox hunter you have to be happier on water than land! Altogether in these two latter years I have spent some twenty-five solid weeks after ferox. What follows is what they have taught me. I realise they are simply an introduction, for, believe me, feroxide has bitten deeper than any other fishing disease of the past and I cannot foresee a cure other than death itself!

A Natural History

Scottish Highland trout can vary in size from three inches to three feet long when fully grown. Traditionally, these larger trout – ferox – were considered to be cannibals. This was the reason given for their survival and large size. Modern research, however, tends to suggest that there is more to it than simply this. Ferox are very likely a sub-species, a breed apart. For well over a century, their colour and their shape has attracted attention. Thornton wrote about ferox in 1804, St John in 1878, Stoddart in 1886, Colquhoun in 1888, Malloch in 1910 and MacKenzie in 1924. All these men have appreciated the beauty and rarity of ferox. They are still fish to present a massive challenge. A recent authority said, 'it is probable that upwards of a million brown trout are caught each season in Scotland, but usually less than five notable ferox in a year are reported'.

The typical ferox is heavily marked with large black spots, covering almost the entire flank of the fish, placed over a background of burnished gold. However, there is considerable variation. Male ferox tend to have bigger heads and obvious teeth with an often kyped jaw. Females have smaller, neater heads. The flesh of a typical ferox – for those who could consider eating such a beast – is a deep scarlet orange.

Their homes are deep, glacial lakes set amidst acid rocks and peat-surrounded countryside. The lochs are generally treeless as severe wave action often allows little vegetation to develop. It is a very low productivity environment and on the surface it is surprising that very big fish like ferox could survive there. Ferox spawn in the deep water of river entries and there is some migration towards there in late October.

Food, of course, is the key to ferox, in Scotland at least. And the food of the ferox is almost invariably the char. The preferred size is possibly about a third of their own body length and for the angler this indicates trolling a dead char of something around eight to twelve ounces. Char are important because they are a shoaling fish and, therefore, there is a constant turnover of weak, sick and dying members. Big ferox are not particularly efficient predators and do not display the cunning of perch or pike. Char present an easy target to feed upon. There are ferox in Loch Lomond which does not contain char, but possibly here powan fulfil this role. On Loch Ness, salmon smelts are also a probable addition to the ferox larder.

Their homes are deep glacial lakes.

Certainly, ferox waters without char are very rare indeed. All other fish species tend to be irrelevant to the ferox. The char is the essentiality. The lakes also have to be one hundred hectares or over. Any less than this and there are probably not enough char to sustain a ferox population.

Scientists believe that in mineral enriched waters, trout grow fast and do not live long. They tend to burn out at a young age. These cold, mineral poor waters, however, seem to produce trout that live and grow over a number of years. A normal trout grows quickly to its third or fourth year and then declines. By five or six it is an old fish and probably dies aged six or seven. Ferox display a similar growth in early life but this continues often with bumper growth between the seventh and ninth years. Significant growth can often continue up until even the sixteenth year. The point of 'ferox growth' – that is when what seem to be ordinary trout take off – can vary, and some lochs have slower rates of growth and produce generally smaller ferox.

Although the ferox probably stops growing between fourteen and sixteen years old it is very probable that they can live for a while after this, much in the way of roach, bream and carp. Whether they live quite as long as these species is, however, doubtful.

The keys to ferox, therefore, are that firstly they must live longer than the normal brown trout. Some of this is luck, some of it is aided by hereditary factors. Secondly, the increased metabolic demands mean a need for a small prey fish. It is fortunate for ferox and for the angler that char, and to a lesser extent trout, provide an abundant food source for them. It can be seen, therefore, that

Cold, mineral poor waters.

longevity and char, the survivors of the retreating ice-cap of the last ice age, are essential factors in the ferox population.

A Sixteen Pound Ferox from Loch Lomond

Barrie Rickards

Time colours everything, sometimes with a fine patina, sometimes with varnish. This note is probably in the former category, but as I write much later in time than the actual event, the patina may not be fully accurate. If this is the case, I apologise: it is sure that I recall that day with a rosy glow for the best of reasons. Hugh Reynolds and I had gone north for a few days in my old Morris 1000 van. I do remember Hugh, when he came to do his spell behind the wheel, was staggered to see the road flashing by beneath his feet. We were to join others to do a survey for a boat hire out from the west bank. To cut a long story short we tried many locations, catching the odd pike here, the odd pike there, noting likely spots and the time taken to get there. We eventually produced a detailed report and I do hope it was acted upon. Because I never heard another word and I have not a clue whether they developed the idea further. Perhaps they just did not like my report.

Conditions over those few days were rather good – essentially high pressure with a nice wind, plenty of ripple and a fair bit of sun. I recall Ron Felton looking rather pink towards the end of the stay! Eventually we fetched up at the very northern end of the loch, at Ardlui, and fished the shallow bay east of the river mouth – an area I had experience of from previous years. Hugh and I were in a flat, concrete-bottomed, aluminium barge. This really was a quite excellent craft from which to fish. One could kneel on the gunwhales without tilting it an inch from the horizontal! We anchored up the two boats close to the mouth of the bay, Hugh and I now in the tub, the rest in the rather plush cabin cruiser. Fish came thick and fast, the best being one of fifteen pounds to Ron Felton, but the average was probably seven or eight pounds.

I was aware of the crashing strikes in the rush beds on the far side, but did not take a lot of notice simply because of the sport we were having. I assumed the strikes were caused by pike feeding on toads. A couple of years previously I had seen them on the flooded grass fields hunting toads in deadly fashion. Each pike sat quite still, watching and waiting for a grounded toad to come up for air. The moment this happened the pike would launch itself from up to twenty yards away, taking the poor toad before it swam the twelve inches into the grass and safety.

Eventually our own feeding spell declined and we elected to make a move, so I hitched up the tub to the back of the cruiser and sat back to enjoy the tow. Half-way across the bay the engines spluttered and then stopped. We drifted in deathly silence towards the far bank, eventually pushed against the rushes by the breeze.

Hugh and I needed no further excuse. He mounted a deadbait and lobbed it out into the middle of the bay and then sat back in the sun. I elected to lure fish and picked one of my favourites for shallow weedy waters, the four-inch yellow Gudebrod Sniper (for some reason best known to themselves Gudebrod refuse to reproduce this superlative plug). I flicked it out perhaps thirty-five yards and marvelled at its slow wobble as it came back about a foot deep over roughly four feet of thick weed beds. Its yellow colour was conspicuous. I was just thinking to myself that perhaps it was a shade too garish, too bright, for the sunlit conditions when my thoughts were killed by the sight of a fast travelling shape homing in on the plug. That glimpse, in truth, the merest fraction of a second, I am sure enabled me to be fully prepared for the subsequent thump, for such it was!

The fish hit the lure, and I hit the fish. The result was immediate and spectacular, and it raced some twenty-five yards to my left with its head and shoulders out of the water, cascading water in every direction. This is a funny looking pike I thought. I did not get a lot of time to think for it then turned on a sixpence and powered towards the boat, saw it, turned turtle in a flash and headed for the horizon. For a while I lost a tight line, regaining the doubtful

Barrie's monster – Hugh looks on.

advantage as the fish distanced itself! I knew it was not a pike. At no time did it sound into the weed. Had it done so I doubt if it would have come anywhere near the landing net. It simply adopted the tactics of moving fast over the top of the weed, never leaping at all. I could see it most of the time but couldn't identify it simply because the sunlit, rippled water dappled its body. I didn't have time to think, let alone guess, what it might be.

It tired quite quickly and I rather skull dragged it in, still protesting in spray, across the landing net. As water separated from its flanks, I saw the spots, the colour and saw a great trout. In the boat it proved to be a beautiful colour; a very firm and muscular fish, well hooked. Weighed quickly, we were quite shocked to read the merest hair's breadth over sixteen pounds. I decided to return the fish immediately, though cameras clicked away. I don't think I could ever kill such a fish, not a wild one anyway – and besides, one of the local trout club officials was in the party with us! That last was all the excuse I needed and I slipped it back only to recoil in dismay as it turned and lay on its side. Ron Felton came to its rescue, and mine: 'Pick it up and drop it into the water from about six feet in the air, quickly!' This I did, doubtfully. The fish hit the water and, as if electrified, powered away in foam, disappearing rapidly. Felton grinned a grin of experience.

Identification of salmonids can be difficult and Ron was vaguely wondering whether it was a salmon kelt – though 'well mended' would be a gross understatement! However, photographs sent to Dave Steuart confirmed it almost certainly as a brown trout.

A Brief Encounter at Rannoch Station

A Saturday in April, and the sun took a long time to set after a crisp day. The mountains around the moor showed up stark, snow-capped, and as I walked to the hotel, all manner of bird life sang from the heath. It was lonely, blissful and beautiful but I still had to stand aside for the last train of the weekend, emerging from the hills and pressing along the single track line. The four-coach train stopped at the Rannoch Station and I saw five figures get down before the lonely train trundled on its way into the fast darkening north. As I walked through the gloom I saw them pick up bags and make their own way in the dusk to the tiny hotel alone on the skyline.

I was interested. I enquired about the new arrivals and found they were railworkers from Glasgow, shuttled in to work on the highland track on Sunday, the line's day of rest. It was a Saturday night I would not forget. Things began to happen around 10.00 p.m. when the lads stumbled around the one television set to watch the two teams from Dundee slog it out in a soccer cup tie. Many a dram was downed as many a skill was applauded. It was not much before midnight when the electric magazine was put aside and it was the occasion to talk. 'Ye dunna see games like that one down south.' I stared at ten hostile eyes and drank up slowly. 'Of course you do. Football is brilliant the world over wherever it is played.'

And that was it. Drinks were brought in and we sat until the fire was cold. We agreed that Liverpool might edge past Celtic but sure it was that Rangers could thrash Manchester United. I said there has never been a greater player than Dennis Law, but if George Best had played in Scotland, and loved football more, he would have stayed on the rails and would have eclipsed even him. I denied that Bobby Charlton should have been Scottish or that Jinky Johnston was Jesus Christ resurrected! We argued on and on over which side of the border all the skill was born. After thrashing it out between Jimmy Greaves and Charlie Nicholas, Bobby Moore and Jimmy Baxter, we agreed on a patchwork compromise. We could all agree to laugh, however, at Scottish goalkeepers and, with tears in our eyes, we ascended the stairs of the cold little hotel shivering on the moor.

It was amazing that we should all have been awake so early the next day, but they were off to work and I was to fish so we met again in the dining room at seven. We were noticeably quieter this time and a little later we flooded out into the bleak sunshine to begin our respective days.

I met them again for a quick drink at sundown in the bar as they waited for the night train to take them back to the great footballing city of Glasgow. 'Any luck today?' they asked. 'Not at all,' I replied. 'Better luck yourselves you lads, in Europe next season.' We shook hands and one said that, for a southerner, they decided I knew at least the rudiments of the game. I waved to them till they disappeared out of sight behind the rolling foothills of the mountains and the hotel seemed a quiet place that evening.

Failure on the Gaur

Miller and I began the 1988 ferox season on Rannoch Moor where the River Gaur runs out of Loch Laidon. It is a wild, desolate place and the weather those first days of April was astounding. One minute it would be piercing cold but the next, sunfilled, peachy warm in any hollow that gave shelter from the ever present wind. We almost preferred the days of sleet and stinging rain, for they made us feel so deserving of a hot bath and excellent food.

The river, too, was in ferocious form, tumbling from its high altitude loch

The Gaur – an unruly body of water.

through the moors. As Miller said, it was hardly a river at all in the conventional sense, but more an unruly body of water bursting to be free and pushing along any course to find its way. Sometimes it steadied a while to form a big deep pool, but then at the tail, it would be off once more, all hairy-scary and white water. In places, the body of water broke into numerous winding channels, each one finding its way past strings of islands before rejoining in a foaming pool and belting on again rejuvenated.

To fish the Gaur for a day involved miles of walking with frequent wide detours for swamp or scree face. At times low sweeping cloud would obscure the entire landscape and we would hug the river for security's sake. Snow would fall for some minutes and even form a soft carpet that melted in seconds as the sun forced its way through and the sky turned blue again.

At first we fished in an obvious, and it seems very wrong, fashion. Logic told us to concentrate on those deep pools where the currents threaded round and round dark water. In such weather, with the river almost snow cold, we figured the fish would be deep and near comatose most of the day. We worked, therefore, at getting plug, spoon, fly and even bait down to the ten foot mark, moving them slowly and covering as much ground as possible. We snagged up now and again but hit nothing that moved.

In 1987 the two trout I had taken from the Gaur, small though they were, were both from fast white water. Their capture had surprised me at the time, as had

Spinning the fast water...

... but into what?

their looks. Miniature ferox both, I thought. They were lean, heavily black spotted, already hook-jawed and absolutely wild at getting caught! But, I started to wonder, perhaps they had not been flukes and the landlord of the pub confirmed all suspicions. As far as he knew, most of the fish came in the rapids to small lures. Why this should be so neither Miller nor I could guess at, but, as we've said to each other a million times, the book on the ferox remains to be written and we were happy to change our plans.

A Ferox from the Gaur

That night, as a result, we set to work on our gear. We put fresh six pound line on the spools, rather than the eight and ten pound stuff we used in the pools. The lighter line would give us better range with light lures, greater accuracy and would catch the current less. And, with six pound line, we felt at least some optimism about getting even a good fish to the bank. We hunted through the tackle bags and laid out a glittering selection of small minnows, plugs and spoons. We dug in the damp night, in vain, for worms; the poor acidic moorland held nothing that we could find.

We also decided to approach the river more delicately. We had fished together before and perhaps caused too much disturbance on such clear water

A perfect baby ferox –
hook-jawed, black-spotted and all
aggression – even at less than 1 lb.

I headed off.

with such sensitive fish. Henceforth, we would split up, and stalk in good traditional fashion. We would wear our polaroids, think through every cast and cut out the mechanical flogging fishing of the past days. We went to our beds quite brimfull of hope and I did not fall asleep for a long time, but rather listened to the snipe call and the songs of the far off tumbling river.

Fishing the rapids well was not easy. In places they stretched a hundred yards across and, with wading quite impossible, many of the nooks and crannies amongst the boulders were impossible to reach. Other pockets of water were so small, I doubted if I could get a light spinner down deep enough or quickly enough for a trout to see it and mount an attack. Always I was fearful that either a fish could not see a bait or it would be gone so fast that it would not have time to react. A strong wind made every task more difficult and early on I often had to stop to breathe warmth back into my exposed finger tips. Mid-morning, however, and the sun made frequent warming appearances and through the polaroids showed the devastating ice clarity of the water I was fishing. I saw rocks deep down and plumes of bubbles glittering amongst them. My six-pound line looked like hawser rope from the little spinner and I began to bet the trout would be able to read the writing on its blade even.

These fears were confirmed in devastating fashion, when, two rod lengths out

Battling in fast water.

I spied a trout inches behind the spoon. The fish was pacing the metal perfectly and the distance between the two never varied. Perhaps the trout was curious; perhaps it was escorting the spinner out of harm's way; certainly it never looked like making an attack. At my feet, the fish turned and melted away. Where it went, or how, I just do not know. It simply disappeared, all two, perhaps three, pounds of it. I sat on a rock and I could have cried. I would have done, surely, but for the sound of Miller's voice calling me, far off beyond the next rapids.

I ran to him. He made a heroic sight, battling with a big fish as the sun glittered from behind banked cloud. The fish was ready for netting when I arrived and only after it had been worshipped and returned, did he tell me of the capture. The trout had fallen as we had planned; the lure was a small, black and silver toby; the taking place was the fast water at the head of a pool. Miller reckoned he was working four or five feet down when the rod simply buckled and the line veed away up the rapids. For a fight, he said, it was everything we had come to expect; immense power and speed, sometimes battling deep and four times airborne. The ferox was average for the Gaur and small for the steel water lochs; it weighed a little under seven pounds and Miller just did not know how he would tackle one, three, four or even five times that first ferox's size.

FEROX

Hook-jawed and solid.

We did not know it then, but soon I would be able to tell him how it is to hold a monster over seventy feet of water and feel quite helpless.

In looks, Miller's ferox was impressive. Its fins were massive, sturdy, as powerful as those of some giant tench. Its jaw was hooked and solid as steel. Its shoulders were bull-like and its spots black and bold as a leopard. We lay on our backs in the heather as we talked and in the better weather, a skylark rose up and sang. Life was simply brilliant.

Introducing Humminbird

From the Gaur we moved north to the large lake we named Mansion Loch in deference to the lodge drowned there when the hydroelectric dam raised the levels. Here we were to take to boats and to troll in traditional ferox style. Here too, we had the assistance of the latest in echo sounders – our little Humminbird. There are those who decry electronic help; in many situations I agree, but on a water of vast length and depth, help for the newcomer is essential. The Victorian ferox hunters, after all, had their gillies; Humminbird is the modern equivalent.

Humminbird gave us, first, knowledge of the depth we were fishing over. From all advice we aim to troll between thirty and seventy feet and a recorder is vital for drop offs to a hundred feet or more can occur in a very short space –

[109]

Miller and Humminbird.

literally two boat lengths. Equally, rocks can rise to the very surface in just a few feet, rather in the manner of a cliff face. Really, some Scottish lochs and this one in particular have a bed of utter chaos, quite unlike the more gentle Irish waters.

Secondly, Humminbird is a fish finder. The bed is shown in black and the fish in red. Such is the theory, and generally the practice, but care must be taken. Submerged vegetation of all types – some very old – can give a false red reading. This is generally very close to the bottom, however, and any red well off bottom is almost certainly a fish. Single fish show up well, especially large ones, but most impressive are the banks of char when they are located. The screen can almost be filled with red, it seems, and wherever the boat goes for over a hundred yards, the picture is the same. We did not really expect Humminbird to lead us to the ferox itself – but if she could direct us to its food then we would be well pleased.

The Perfect Fishing Inn

You might well think that the Dick Down exists only in make-believe but you would be very wrong. To the ferox angler it is the land of the lotus-eater and after a while you can hardly bear to consider life apart from it. The place has all things any angler could ever require in plenty. It was even built for sport, as a lodge in late-Victorian Scotland, and it has perched on its hillside now for a century, bringing joy to all who stay to fish and shoot there. The place simply reeks of fish, game and late at night whisky. There is an atmosphere around it and it is as tangible as the sheen along a salmon. The regular Dick Downer knows all this.

The hotel has the most wonderful views of the glen, from the softer east to the west where it rises remorselessly towards the snow-capped peaks that stand guardian over one of the most wonderful lochs in the country. At the foot of the valley runs a river, fast, broad, deep and clear, up which salmon pass from loch into loch. There are pike there too, big ones, and brown trout all beautiful and some big. Deep in the lochs there are char and even perch: something swims for everyman.

Go through the mahogany doors of the hotel and a hallway greets you with

The Dick Down in Edwardian times.

The Dick Down bar – Miller, Reel Screamer, Bailey, Shaunagh, Gordon and Maureen with a record char. A ferox looks on.

brass bell, solid wooden stairs and a tanglewood of antlers. Ring that bell and the host appears; a Welshman in Scotland but never out of place; a man to spill all his knowledge and bubble over with his enthusiasm and his love for the glen. He is a man who will not shut the bar until the very last tale has been told or until every last plan for the coming day has been laid. Never until well past midnight does he close the hotel up and go to his room, passing contented anglers snoring, dreaming, here and there around the building.

His shed is that of a fisherman. Boats and engines, paddles and rowlocks, rods and reels and lines and everything a man could ever need up in these parts. If you want a fly, he's got it, if you need some worms, then he has a tip just up the hill. Fancy a char to troll and simply look in his deep freeze. Food is never a problem. If you need to be up early there will be a flask and something packed up ready. If you are determined to be out late you will know something hot and tasty can be got for you at any time, even after midnight. Come in wet and take a brandy to the great enamelled baths. Come in tired and sleep deep in the soundless Scottish night. If you are a fisherman this is your true home.

One gentleman failed to leave. The lovely Shaunagh told us the tale as eleven

A regular Dick Downer – and 18lb ferox.

o'clock approached and the lamps gleamed on an old photograph by the bar. There, in sepia, a fine looking man held a monstrous ferox at his side. It was majestic. That fish was everything I wanted from this lovely glen. It appeared that the man rejoiced in the hotel and that the great ferox sealed his love affair with it. For decades he stayed at the Dick Down and never actually left it, even in death. Over and over, his shadow made unmistakable by his wide brimmed hat, is seen on the top corridor before turning in to what was his customary room – room 7. I looked at my key lying on the bar. The very same. I looked up to catch Shaunagh's eye, watching for a twinkle of mirth. She was serious. It neared midnight and I took up with me a bottle of the very best malt whisky Dick Down possessed and two glasses.

The moonlight flooded the room as I poured two full measures and placed them carefully by the cup stand. I said my prayers and I got into bed. I heard the hall clock chime midnight, then one and then nothing more. And so it has always been. Still he has not come to talk to me but he will and we will drink the whisky and he will tell me the tale of the ferox. Then the past and the present will hold hands in a place that time has forgotten, so far, to change.

The Dick Down has always been a haven for anglers. I have a book published in 1908 which describes the glen as quite 'an angler's paradise'. The author has nothing but good things to say about the Dick Down.

The regular Dick Downer never thought of changing his clothes for dinner unless he were wet through, the dinner was not supposed to take place until half-past eight and at times it has been known to be as late even as eleven before we sat down to that meal. So it was hardly worthwhile even bothering to change, for nobody but the hardy fisherman ever frequented the inn. I have heard gentlemen at the Inver Hotel in immaculate evening dress discussing the place over their wine – "Dick Down! Ah, yes, a perfectly impossible hole ten miles up the valley!" Probably it would be so to them. But to the good old Dick Downer in his ancient checked shooting suit and flannel shirt and cap bristling with flies, it was a paradise; for where could he get such untrammelled freedom, combined with such excellence of sport?

The Book Has Not Been Written

Miller and I, having encountered so many problems with ferox and found so little help, have coined a favourite phrase: 'the book on ferox has not been written...' It has not, perhaps, yet, but there are clues from the past if one is prepared to dig and delve.

For example, take this piece from Charles St John's book *Wild Sports of the Highlands* written in mid-Victorian England... 'choose the roughest wind your

Choose the roughest water your boat can live in.

boat can live in; fish with a good sized bait not much less than a herring and do not commence your trolling until after two o'clock in the afternoon by which time the large fish seem to have digested their last night's supper, and to be again on the move.' There is a lot of truth in what St John wrote here, the good-sized bait definitely holds true. A good wind is definitely excellent. An afternoon appears to be a better time than morning.

John Colquhoun wrote his book *The Moor and the Loch* in 1851. In it he devotes a whole chapter to trolling for the salmo-ferox as he calls them. He was obviously a successful ferox man and gives serious clues to the best time of the ferox season: 'the best time of year for the salmo-ferox is the end of April/May and the beginning of June. They are dormant all July and August. Although much more shy than in spring, they sometimes take pretty fair in September. A small bait is generally most successful in these months. The large ones lie farther from the shore than earlier in the season. Many of the best worth hooking even haunt the middle of the loch at this time of the year. I killed two last September, 1850, in mid-loch, which weighed twelve and a half and twelve pounds. Some of the Loch Awe fishing guides suggested to me that the partiality of the ferox for deep water then might be occasioned by the pike driving the small trout from the shallows and that the ferox follow the shoals into the deep to prey upon them.'

Bailey and a good sized bait.

Undoubtedly, most ferox anglers – those that there are – have found the early season to be the best.

Finally, Ernest Briggs wrote *Angling and Art in Scotland* in Edwardian England. He certainly captured the glamour of the ferox hunt. 'The whole hotel seemed to be suffering from ferox on the brain. Were an angler fortunate enough to get a run from a fish which might, possibly be one of these monsters, and mention the fact at dinner, he was looked upon with awe – considered quite a hero for several days, the event having to be recounted many times before an enquiring and appreciative audience.'

He also included a story of ferox, which, had Miller and I read it earlier could have put two fish on the bank for us. 'It would be about ten o'clock when I was starting to row in the loch and very soon after Charles was putting out the trolls. A fish came on one of the rods with a great rush and away went the reel. While I was winding in the spare rod, Charles was playing the big fish. And just then, she made a great run and what did he do – he must catch the handle of his reel in his watch guard. Indeed yes! As any individual would be telling you – snap went the steel trace as she might be a threat and the fish – she was away!'

Notice that phrase, the steel trace! Nowhere had we read of using wire for ferox but if we had read that chapter earlier two ferox might have been under

The line severing capacity of a good trout's jaws.

our belt. On consecutive days on Mansion Loch big fish were hooked and lost. Both times we had suffered bite offs – with the baits and a couple of inches of line being taken. Obviously, these big trout have jaws as tough as a pike's that give nylon line very little chance indeed. We needed no further telling. Our nylon traces were substituted, for fine wire. The past obviously has much to tell us.

The Fight of a Wild Fish

At the first Norfolk Angling Conference in May 1988, that excellent carp man Tim Paisley, mentioned how a virgin carp had fought so hard that it exhausted itself and could have died from the stress. As Tim said, 'that carp was fighting for its life as far as the fish itself knew'. Indeed, without any previous experience of capture, the first fight for any fish must be especially traumatic.

Very few game fish live to fight another day. Virtually all salmon and most trout are virgin. Perhaps that partly explains the spirit they show, for certainly some often-caught coarse fish reach the stage of hardly fighting at all. A certain Bayfield tench springs to my mind from way back in 1975. First caught on 18 June he fought like a demon. On 20 June, he still had a bit of the tiger in him. 23 June and he plugged around for a while but on 27 June he came in with barely a fin raised in anger. I do not really believe that tench was physically tired; rather I think that he had learnt the game and knew how to accept his fate. He had realised he was *not* fighting for his life.

I take these considerations very seriously. The quests discussed in this book are large noble fish, most of which if not all, have never seen a hook before. Some, I realise, have reached a vulnerable old age and I do not tamper with them lightly. Take a ferox – a magnificent cannibal brown trout – perhaps three feet long, probably more than fifteen years old. I could no more accept killing him than I could a leopard, a panda or a white rhinoceros – all of them magnificent beasts. Any thinking man must care for them all.

How, then, should a large, virgin fish best be played? Quite obviously, the tackle used should be well chosen, well balanced and as strong as possible. Any possible flaws or weaknesses must be checked out lest hooks and lines be left on a fish allowed to break free. I have read of methods in the angling press designed to play big carp on two-pound line or even less. On such gear the battle is bound to be protracted. The carp must suffer. The whole concept is quite wrong, immoral even. Fine tackle for fine fish? Rubbish. Sense and the right gear must prevail.

Correct tackle inspires confidence during the battle itself. With the big fish, the angler must be firm. He should not be brutal and haul the fish in as this can harm the lips or jaws of the quarry, but he has got to be master in the fight. He must not play a fish over long and tax its strength but bring it to the net as soon as is practicable. A landed fish should be beaten but only tired, not exhausted or destroyed.

On the land, exultation or greed for photographs should not take over. A fish should always be laid on wet sacking or nets. Photographs must be taken then and there whilst a fish is still too tired to struggle when being held. A squirming fish has to be gripped hard or dropped – both as dangerous as each other. I do not believe a fish should ever be sacked to await better light for photography. Use a flash at night or fill-in flash for dusk, dawn, and gloomy winter days. Damn the photograph album if a fish's well-being is at stake.

Even after returning a fish, after-care could still be necessary. To leave a tired, big fish to its own devices in the water could be fatal. Check it is not going to turn belly up, hold it stable if you feel there is such a danger. Nurse a fish an hour or all night if you must, but do not let it just take its chance through idleness or apathy. As more anglers are born, as methods and tackle improve and as pollution spreads, the pressures increase on big, magnificent fish. Make sure we all deserve the gifts and glories they offer.

After-care may be necessary.

£150.00 per Ounce

'I should think,' said Miller 'that this little blighter has cost me half a month's salary!' He held the tiny fish aloft where it wriggled and kicked in the sunshine. We did not want to put it back – you see it was the very first char either of us had ever seen at that moment, and so we could not bear to let it go. Like scallywags out of school, we kept it in the bailing bucket for an hour or so till the heat seemed to be getting the better of its little, cold-water body and then we slipped it back. In an instant, it had melted to the depths of forty feet from whence it had come. After that we drifted home in euphoria; four ounces – if that – of char had made us the happiest of men. Thirty-pound pike or carp are one thing; four ounces of char can be almost comparable.

After all, what we had held in our hands was as near as possible to the living fossil, to the visible proof of the tumultuous times that built this most awe inspiring beloved region. This tiny fish, we felt, linked us to its ancestors, to the times past when the glaciers began to move and to gouge out the sheer-sided, impressively deep lochs we now know. When the ice melted, the chasms filled with water, icy then and cold still, that proved happy for the char that began to colonise. Today, all over the highland region, the char still flourish in their many sub-species – some of which are only yet coming to the light of day. And, as you

[119]

The Mansion before the level was raised.

might expect, with a fish of such antiquity and rugged history, catching them is often no simple matter.

Believe me, that single little char had caused us a great deal of sweat. April, and it was not a problem to find the shoals on the depth recorder. Indeed, sometimes they were packed so densely that the red dots signifying fish merged to become black smudges that indicated almost an impenetrable mass. At times these shoals were to cover areas the size of football pitches. Of course, we were after ferox but what fisherman can resist a challenge? Did not Richard Walker catch the gudgeon at Redmire when sport was slow there in the 1950s?

We dropped worms to the char and occasionally one came back nibbled, lumpy like a walking stick. We jigged baby spinners to them and nothing happened. I couldn't compute how many thousand char saw our baits without giving a proper take – until I took off the worm and tied on a size sixteen Red Ant for Miller. The result was our fabulous little fish. After that breakthrough, catching the char became slightly easier. Jigging flies began to take a measure of fish, including specimens of near on a pound in weight. At times it seemed that a shoal would catch fire and half a dozen fish would come out in five minutes.

[120]

Then again, it would be hard going for a single fish and at times they would prove just impossible.

The Hunt for the Char

Finding the char shoals, we hoped, would lead us to the ferox. Char formed the basis of the ferox diet and we felt it unlikely that on such large waters ambush would be a practical way for the ferox to hunt. Rather each char shoal must attract its attendant predators that follow on behind, wolf-like after sheep. Ferox experts are nearly as rare as the great fish themselves, but those men with knowledge that we did contact backed up our belief – albeit with some hesitation. Let us say that at least our hypothesis seemed a likely one to all.

In April, we were staggered by several aspects of the char shoals. One thing that struck us was their size. An area two hundred yards square could be thick with fish at depths between thirty and one hundred plus feet. I cannot possibly imagine how many char would be in such a shoal, but several hundreds of thousands cannot be an over estimate.

During the spring, two areas had been particularly frequented by large shoals. The favourite had been around the site of the old shooting lodge and its grounds,

Into another world.

flooded by the hydroelectric scheme after the War. The drowned, destroyed buildings and rhododendron gardens would seem to provide some food and shelter from undertow and predators and char were very often found there in vast quantities. The second area was the dam itself. Again the recorder showed a great deal of rubble on the floor of the loch which presumably attracted the shoals. As a dam lay to the east it was also the ultimate focal point of the prevailing westerly winds. The char appeared to like the rougher water and probably aspects of the undertows of which we, in detail, could know very little.

Both these areas were at the bottom, deeper end of the loch. The water there seemed slightly warmer, too, than at the western end where it was shallower and received the rivers and burns of snow-melt from the mountains.

A particular fascination was the speed and the distance that a char shoal could travel. A shoal located in the evening would almost always be gone by the next morning. An area thick with char in the morning, like the mansion bank, could be devoid by the late afternoon. Indeed, there might be no fish within a mile of it, so complete would be the evacuation. It was this that convinced us the ferox moved with the shoal; little energy would be spent for surely all the fish drifted on the undertows and the currents. And if the ferox were not to move with their dinner, it could be a great while before the dishes reappeared over them again.

We both felt that the presence of a boat above the char unsettled them at less than fifty feet. An engine probably made their unease worse. The water is truly glacier clear and like little birds the char seemed to be ever aware on the fin. After two or three trolls around and through a shoal, the recorder showed them quite distinctly breaking up and starting to spread away. We wondered how the boat affected the ferox too, remembering the advice of older writers – choose the roughest water your boat can live in.

It was, therefore, with some confidence of finding char that I returned in late May. I was struck by how low the loch lay, fifteen feet below its April levels, but I streamed happily to the dam. There were no fish. To the mansion. Up and down. I could see its outline on the recorder. No char. A whole day more I spent on the lower loch; I found nothing but sparsely scattered trout and went to the hotel a sad and sorry man.

Then it was that Gordon, the landlord, suggested a journey to the top end of the loch where the shallows lay and where the char just might have migrated. Even on full throttle, against the slightest of wind, with just one angler aboard, it would take not less than two hours to reach the furthest, shallowest arm, but my mind was made up to explore. I could really do nothing else.

Early morning, 1 June, and I began the assembly of the gear. The engine had to be double checked for such a voyage and three gallons of fuel were prepared as the sun began to look out through the mist. A little wine, a smattering of food, all the tackle a man might possess and I was on the track up to the boat. As I looked down on the loch, I knew I was to be fortunate; even at high altitude there was no wind and the sun seemed closer, more brilliant and warmer. Within minutes I was settled at the helm, chugging on, happy, making a wide wake to the west.

For seven miles, the sounder screen showed nothing but vast depth and few fish, but as I found the mouth to the final arm, I sensed a change. There, cloaked off by rising mountains that still kept a little of their winter snows, lay another world. It was silent there, and secret and seemed to be waiting for my presence in the strangest of ways. I was an intruder into a forbidden place, I cut the engine and made my way silently on the oars.

The sounder showed the bottom in steep ascent. A hundred feet, eighty feet, seventy feet and within a hundred yards a steady thirty feet pock-marked with depressions of forty or fifty feet. Most exciting of all, the arm, the whole mile of it, was alive with fish! I rode on an erratic course, but wherever I went, the red banks of char showed and led me on, ever thickening to the head of the loch.

I landed there, on a beach, that I swear had felt no other boots for a year at least and wandered a mile along a mountain path. It led me into a corrie, to a water filled with small trout and in minutes I had my trolling baits in the bag and could return to the big loch.

Something wonderful had happened; though there was cloud over the western peaks, blue sky mirrored off the water. The warmth of the sunburst had brought an insect hatch and the arm dimpled everywhere to rising fish. For the whole of the afternoon I caught char on the fly. There were fish to a pound. Fish of staggeringly different colouration and shapes and all of them beautiful. I had done more than find the char. I was catching them, wallowing in them, drunk with them. I forgot ferox for once and only a sudden chill wind made me glance at my watch. God, Gordon would be coming to look for me in only two more hours. My day had melted away and, a wildly happy man, I steamed away from the steadily setting sun. In July I knew I would return up the arm, to live there just as long as it might take to land my ferox. From the journey down the loch, I began to lay my plans for the return.

They were, of course, frustrated. Once more, in July and August, the char changed their habits for the high summer. Now, it seemed that the shoals had utterly fragmented and split into many, small groups spread everywhere around the loch. On calm evenings, shoals of fifteen to twenty char could be seen dimpling everywhere on the water. Possibly now there was fly life the mass concentrations had divided to capitalise on the relative summer food bonanza.

This, of course, frustrated our main ferox technique. Now we could not find a char shoal and work around it. Now we had to accept the ferox could be spread as thinly as the char and trolling miles was the only real key to success. There

The British record char – at nearly 5lb.

were still areas where the char did gather in some intensity. Humminbird showed us these locations where we did put in a fair degree of effort. For some reward.

Our Trolling Techniques

I must stress that the more we learn the less we seem to know! Miller in particular is an expert boat angler and has specialised in bream and pike, both afloat. Ferox trolling is, however, a quite new experience.

First, the boat must be as stable as possible. It must weather quite heavy winds at all times of the year with the ever present possibility of a real storm blowing up. It must easily accommodate two anglers with a great deal of gear around them. There will also be times when a third angler takes to the boat. An engine is an absolute essential for the ferox troller. It must be able to troll at very low speeds indeed. Reverse gear is also almost essential both to re-trace steps over snags to free lures and also to chase fish should this prove to be necessary. Absolute reliability can also in certain situations save your life. Storms do blow up out of nowhere and the engine that will not start or which fades and eventually cuts is the worst possible equipment to have in such a situation. Extra

[124]

petrol – at least one can full – should also always be taken afloat. Never forget the oars. It is tempting to think everything can be done on the engine but there will be times the thing refuses to fire. Do not forget the rowlocks and do ensure that they fit the boat before setting out. Never forget either the bailing bucket or the life-jackets. It could prove fatal if both these pieces of equipment are forgotten. These are very large waters and must not be tampered with.

Boat rod rests are essential. They can be bought from any good tackle dealer but do remember to screw them very tightly on to the boat's sides. The pressure exerted on them when the fish is hooked or a snag is encountered is enormous and at almost £10.00 each you do not want to see them disappear over the side into a hundred feet of water. I have already talked about echo sounders and I will only add here that to tackle such large waters without an echo sounder is quite foolish indeed. Finally, most of these Scottish lochs are, in fact, too deep to anchor in. The method is trolling and it is generally only possible to fish by keeping on the move or possibly drifting with the wind.

The question of rods is an interesting one. Many Scotsmen tend to use short six-to eight-foot rods when afloat. However, we do not really agree with this. The rods we use are powerful pike-type weapons of two and a half or three pounds test curve. We feel these give far better control over big fish. Moreover they will hold the baits further out from the sides of the boat and this, particularly, we feel is a very important point. The more ground that can be covered the better. Certainly we do not feel that a long rod is an encumbrance in a boat and tangles are very rare in any case.

The question of reels is easily solved. Multipliers are simply a must. For most of my life I have been a fixed spool or centre pin man but here I appreciate just how essential the multiplier is. The line must be fifteen-pounds breaking strain and no less. There is much heavy work for it to do and frequent changes are going to be necessary. Line twist is a major problem. Nowadays after two bite-offs, Miller and I always use thin wire traces up from the bait.

The bait, or one of them at least, is almost always an artificial lure. Almost anything can take a fish: Big 'S' plugs have worked; Rapala lures are successful; Tobys – specially silver and bronze and copper ones – are also favourites; a big fish from Loch Laggan was recently taken on a small Mepps. In short, most plugs, spoons and spinners are worth an extended trial.

One rod will nearly always be baited up with a dead fish. Char are the best, but small trout come a close second. We use three trebles on the wire trace – one in the head, one in the belly and a third in the tail. Live baits could also work at certain times, we feel. All baits – natural or artificial – are weighted. Barrels and Bullets are the preferred weights and we vary the amount according to the year and the depth of the troll.

At the start of the troll we stop the boat and let plenty of line out. We like to feel the lure hit bottom and then we know we are off to a good start. Thereafter we vary the trolling speed from very slow, to slow to quicker and even sometimes with short fast bursts. When trolling dead baits we even stop the boat a while to let them sink completely. By doing this it is possible to snag up to ninety odd feet. When trolling we rarely take a dead straight line but rather adopt a zigzag course along the preferred depths. These depths are generally around the twenty-five to fifty-five foot contour but one four-pound, two-ounce fish was taken at over a hundred feet. It is for this reason that dead baits can often work very well, by getting exceptionally deep to the fish in cold or rough weather.

The ferox strike can be confused with hooking the bottom and you think 'oh no, not again!' With a lure, the fish is instantly on but with a dead bait it is often best, if possible, to give the taking fish time. It is very exciting to see line run out and too soon a strike can easily lose a fish as they do take some while to engulf the bait properly. Certainly the first take we ever had to a dead bait we missed by striking quite a while too soon and the fish was not even pricked.

The best conditions have traditionally been rough. The wind whips up

Ideal trolling conditions – a swell and subdued light.

undertows which force the ferox into movement. It is safest to troll first into the wind so that if there should be any problem with the motor at least you can row home with the wind behind you rather than into your face. In occasional calms, we have found it pays to take to the oars as they make less noise and disturbance than the petrol engine. Always beware of the line around the propeller. Tangle will stop the engine and could be dangerous in rough weather.

The obvious areas to investigate are where the char shoals mass. After the summer break-up of the char shoals all the normal areas are worth attention. Bays, snags, drowned forests, drop offs, islands – all features demand the attention of the troller. However, ferox could be anywhere and as the Victorians proved two hundred miles trolling is about par for the course for each ferox. Even with echo sounders I do not think things have changed tremendously.

The ferox can nip a bait and simply pluck it. The take need not be full-blooded. It therefore pays to watch the rod tips very carefully for any untoward movement. If you should see one keep working that area. My biggest fish, hooked and unfortunately lost, was actually taken on its fourth attack. The previous three had been half-hearted affairs but then finally he summoned up the energy or the confidence to smack properly into the bait.

There is no doubt that night trolling is a very exotic possibility. As far as I am

Miller considers a night troll.

aware very few people have yet done it. On one night Miller and I trolled very small live baits around the shoreline when the water was calm. Fish were dimpling everywhere and on one occasion, a hundred yards along the bank, there was a splashy take in amongst small trout. Obviously we cannot comment further because so much work needs to be done on this.

Never before have I realised how fine the divide between success and failure is. To catch a ferox many cogs have to mesh. Firstly the weather must be right and this of course is in the lap of the gods. Secondly you need to find the food shoals, the char. The recorder does that for you. Next you have to choose the right baits. Fourthly you must troll them at the right speeds. Fifthly you must troll them at the right depths. Sixthly you must go over or close to a ferox. Seventh, you must hope he is hungry – he probably only feeds once or twice a week so you must be lucky. Eighth, you must hope the gear is sound after hours of chafing on rocks and underwater obstructions. Last of all you must pray that the hooks stay in a jaw that is as bony as any stag's antler.

The Lesson of the Old Bridge to Skye

In the early days I was insistent. Why cannot we get to the bank? Why cannot we fish, as some can, paternoster? Why cannot we even drift – anything we know all about? Well, we tried it once. Things seemed very favourable indeed. The weather, for a change, was calm. We had located char very close to the bank. We could land the boat with ease and I had my way.

In minutes we whipped up four paternoster rigs and had trout out there in the danger zone. The attempt was a disaster – a fiasco. The loch, calm though it appeared, had an undertow to shame the Trent. Two-ounce bombs bounced. Three-ounce bombs still could not hold. Whatever the weight, the whole rig was dashed inshore, into the rocks, into tangles in minutes. Everything we did was futile and when we went afloat once more and found the shoal of char, and presumably any attendant ferox, long gone, we felt doubly foolish. Since, I have remained afloat. Other than to stalk rising fish close inshore, I doubt if I will change my mind greatly in the future.

Obviously these underwater currents are quite out of any of my experience. Not the largest broad builds up swells like these. In the big gravel pits, islands take years to disappear; on waters like these, they would be gone in weeks, I guess.

The big ferox lochs are often seven or more miles long, massively deep and lie in glens that channel and intensify the wind down them. In minutes a breeze can throw up a ripple and a wind can create waves. What storms can do, the few

Winding from the moor, my salmon stream.

Calvin Warnes with a beauty from the Flyfisher's Lake.

Dog poised, the angler fishes intent.

The Flyfisher's Lake in December.

The start of Jim Tyree's run to the moon!

Miller with a fish from the Murky.

The lure of the barbel – a Wensum giant.

The Wye shallows sing of barbel.

In the boat on Mansion Loch.

April, Ferox and the Highlands.

times I have seen them, frightens the life out of me. I feel sure this is why the char are so mobile. The water is constantly on the move and the shoals follow. The Humminbird seems to suggest that more territorial trout shelter behind rocks, and gullys or any water break.

And how strong are these currents? Only the Bridge to Skye can truly attest. The road is an ancient one, winding over the hills in a rough north-westerly direction towards the Outer Isles. It was surfaced for motor cars and kept in commission until the 1950s. Then, the loch it traversed was raised by a dam to provide hydroelectric power, and a new, grand, trunk road was led around the glen. So, for nearly thirty years, the old road has been six to ten feet below the surface of the loch. Look at it now, in 1988, after weeks of drought, with levels desperate, low enough to reveal what the undertows have done.

For a little way below the normal water-line, the road is intact. The further out you venture, the more twisted and contorted the old road becomes. Half-way out into the loch, the road is like a snake trying to discard its skin. It writhes, throwing off the tarmac which has already been slaked away in slabs and slivers yards long. The ancient stone bridges are all but stripped of the more modern surfacing and stand there arched and completely still, but bared by the pulling waters. The bridges say it all. Never believe these places are still, not even

Like a snake throwing off its skin . . .

. . . the ancient stone bridge all but stripped.

beneath the most mirrored of surfaces. Forget the bank, forget the methods of the lowlands. Nothing is similar, really, so you must be afloat and follow where the char go, like, I suspect, the ferox themselves.

The Great Fight on Mansion Loch

A wild night continued into morning. Throughout the dawn, the wind had got up, risen and risen until the pines began to moan before it. Wet had followed, driven in from the Atlantic, ploughing, smashing into the peaks and spilling curtains of rain down the glen. The wave had built up down the loch until white horses reared high, and I was forced to flee to the sanctuary of the dam. It was rough, very rough there, but fishable and I was glad still to be afloat. Heavy weather indeed.

I could do little but patrol the area and found at once a shoal of char in the band between forty to seventy feet, lying just off the pumping station. Around and around the shoal I trolled and, if anything, the weather worsened around me. It was blowing more than half a gale now, but my mind was firmly on the job of working the baits and keeping the boat afloat and roughly on its course.

At around 11 o'clock, one rod tip bounced hard. I reckon my bait was perhaps forty feet down over the recorded fifty to fifty-five feet of water. It could not have been the bottom that hit my char! It was most probably a sunken tree or bush I guessed – or a fish. I reeled in. The char seemed untouched. Would that the dead fish could speak! I let it go down again and continued the troll.

A second time I crossed the place and there was another tap. A third time and a similar knocking and twenty minutes later, at ten minutes past midday a fourth time I was broadside to the waves off the pumping station. At the same place, the rod dipped and stayed down. I stopped the boat and moved it back to the obstruction. I gave line. Nothing happened. I held the boat steady. After a minute, just as I was sure I had caught the bottom, line hissed off into the greyness beneath. The spool simply span and I knew at last the char was taken.

The reel stopped. The line lay on the water. And still I held the boat as best I could against the swell. Watching, praying, desperate all the while, and then, again, something beneath began to move with solemn purpose. I clicked on the spool and wound down to the disappearing line. Everything grew tight and I hit the fish with all the might of the rod in my hands.

For that second I believed it was the bouldered bottom again. But when the line zipped through the waves at the stern of the boat and off into the waste waters at the Mansion Loch I knew that ferox, like lightning, had struck this once. Very soon affairs were desperate. I had never felt a fish of this power and the manner of the fight before. Imagine a carp and gigantic barbel fused together and you are close. The runs, even though the fish was deep, were breathtaking, forcing me to follow into the swell. Soon I was motoring after the fish – trying to keep the line tight, trying to steer the boat and keep a proper speed behind the fish. I had not been able to reel in the other two outfits and one caught in the propeller. At times, the engine began to falter and I knew that if it should die there was no way I could play the fish and work the oars in waters such as these.

Heaven knows how many times the line had dropped slack and all contact had been lost, until it had ripped tight and my heart began its beat again. Yet I was over the fish now. Rain was teeming down. There was as much water in the boat, nearly, as without. The engine stuttered, and inside my one-piece suit I sweated and swore. My back ached but I was nearly there. I began to sense it; no fish could last long against a three-pound test curve carbon rod, fifteen-pound line and direct vertical pressure. I glanced at the screen of the Humminbird: I was over one hundred and fourteen feet. Something caught my eye. There was a dot of red and black at fifty-five feet. There, in vision, was my ferox! I simply stared, aghast. I was sure he would be mine now.

I kneeled on the bench and pumped and pumped, but still he would dive and line would be lost. I saw him at sixty feet and then again at seventy feet. I watched the missile plummet to the bottom of the screen. At 12.31 p.m. The rod suddenly fell slack in my hands and a fast moving speck disappeared from my vision.

In despair, I worked the limping boat back to the base and my eyes were closed by the rain. My dull brain sought solution. Not enough line given on the second run? The gyrations of the boat? The constant changes of pressure on the hook points that had worn themselves free?

Then elation filled me. This was no Gaur six-pound fish. There are not many men to have battled twenty minutes with a giant brown trout. I was, at last, doing things half right. I had come so damn close and I knew I would not turn back now.

John MacDonald's Angling Diary

John MacDonald is the United Kingdom's most successful ferox angler and his partnership with Bob Tarr has accounted for more sensational ferox landings than at any time since the 1880s. He began his angling with coarse fish, which has helped him greatly with his trolling techniques and understanding of big predators. His training as an engineer has also been instrumental in the design and application of trolling devices.

Bob Tarr with a huge fish.

In 1980 he moved from the Glasgow area to the Highlands and in 1984, whilst piking, he took wild browns of four and six pounds. So geography and inspiration combined and the search for the British ferox record began.

Here I feel privileged to look into John's angling diary. The following is part of a most sensational record. Remember these fish are utterly wild and have no stew pond origins. They are as natural to the Highlands as the very eagles. Indeed like those predators of the air, ferox are the ultimate hunters of the deep.

16 March 1985
Weight 14lb 8oz. Weather – strong westerly, very heavy snow all day, 0°C. Water rough, coloured, 3°C. Bait Big 'S'. This trout was my first double and remains my biggest so far. Out of all of the fish I have seen this must be the most beautiful. It also fought the hardest, taking a full thirty minutes to land as it continually dived under the boat, giving plenty of anxious moments. Bob and I were very lucky to be fishing that day as snow storms blocked most of the roads and it took over an hour to drive from Inverness to Drumnadrochit. But after that the road cleared. The trout was the only fish of the day and was caught about 4.00 p.m. We were both soaked and miserable, but we forgot the weather when the fish was hooked.

7 June 1985
Weather – sunny, 13°C. Water choppy, 11°C. Weight 16lb 8oz and 12lb. Baits spoon and Big 'S'. These fish were caught at the end of a week that 'Ballantines' (the whisky company) had arranged as a monster hunt in an attempt to break the British record. The loch had been fished twenty-four hours a day for a week before we came, with top anglers coming from all over Scotland, but nothing had so far been caught. We were the last hope on the last day and fortunately we let nobody down. The 16lb 8oz fish was landed at midday and was thirty-four inches long with an eighteen-inch girth. When the fish was landed after about ten minutes battle, we noticed the organiser of the week driving alongside the loch. We therefore decided to take the fish to him. We half filled the boat with water and headed across the loch. Needless to say the organisers were amazed. They would never have believed us if we said we had put the fish back so we returned it in front of them. The 12lb fish was landed on the same day at 6.00 p.m. and measured thirty-four inches long with a sixteen inch girth. This fish was returned immediately and they believed us – as they would with one look at the photographs. We took scales from both fish to have them aged. The sixteen and a half pounder was aged at seven years and the twelve pounder at only five years. However I do know that scale counts are not very accurate and these fish could be older.

Just look at this tail.

27 April 1986
Weight 11lb. Weather – sunny with a light westerly, 13°C. Water, low, clear and calm, 6°C. Bait a doctored plug. Again I was on my own. This trout was quite drab colourwise but it was as fat as a pig with a twenty-inch girth and only twenty-six inches long. Its belly I could feel was full of small fish. This trout was hooked at about thirty feet down and fought well for something like ten minutes.

20 September 1986
Weight 14lb. Weather – strong westerly, 8°C. Water rough, 10°C. Bait plug. I was on my own when I caught this trout. It was the longest ferox of all my catches being thirty-six inches long with only a fifteen-inch girth. But despite the shovel-like tail it fought very poorly which was just as well as the very heavy weather made boat control most difficult.

19 March 1988
Weight 11lb 10oz. Weather – showers and a still westerly, 11°C. Water rough and dirty, 3°C. Bait spoon. A marvellous fish caught on Loch Ness.

Fat as a pig – but piscatorial beauty.

The longest of feroxes.

A sensational Ness fish.

August Epitaph

I must leave. Another three weeks has passed. A four-pound Mansion Loch fish landed and two bigger ones lost have been the total reward for tremendously hard work and still I just cannot explain the love I feel for this place. The fish, I know, are exceptional, so too is everything in the world here. I love the mountains, the way they are snow-capped in the spring and green now in the summer. I love their sheer rocky sides and the way the sun sets behind them. I love the slant of the colours and the shifting rays of light – cold gold and warm gold, burnished all the while. I love the glens that lead off from the water, the tracks that wind into the hills along brightest clearest streams of snow-melt water. I love the clouds that wreath the heather and race across the mountain tops spreading huge shadows as they go. I love the buzzards hanging there – soundless, soaring, just sometimes seeming to call my name. I love the black cock and the ptarmigan. Even eagles frequent my glen. Didn't Miller see one on his first night and shout in terror, 'God! Help! Isn't that a pterodactyl?' I love to see the deer on the highest ground beneath the snow-line in the spring and at almost 3,000 feet in the summer escaping the heat and the flies. Stags peer from the skyline as the hinds eat. I love the air – its purity through and through and the light that is warmth itself and clarity indeed.

I climbed a mountain overlooking the loch and there I saw it in its proper setting. Every point of the compass and mountains and glens and more lochs stretched away from me. Adventure, exploration and experimentation are endless things here. Now, sad though I am to leave, I am already planning a return at the end of the season when the urge to spawn might have led the ferox to the big feeder streams. I do know, whatever happens, I will not give up on this country or on this fabled fish. There is no such thing as ultimate success and knowledge here. It is one of the few places in the British Isles where the challenge will always exist. No man will ever be able truly to say that he knows ferox.

5
At the End

Thoughts

This, I suppose, is a book that could be seen as a history of failure by some. I failed to catch the huge pike of the Flyfisher's Lake, the Boathouse Lake's big one, a Wye barbel and a really large ferox.

I do not view it like this. After all, the book is a part record of the most thrilling two years of my angling life. I was in constant quest for really worthwhile fish that I knew would astound me should they be banked. I also learned a great deal. Trolling is now second nature to me and I believe that I almost understand the massive lochs – which is something! My next mission to the Wye, I doubt will be abortive either. My knowledge of estate lake carp has been greatly expanded and I have thought evermore about my pike fishing.

There have been some great adventures, I have met some fascinating people, and there have been moments of high drama – not least at the very moment this book was being finished. I had returned from Scotland with two-, four- and five-pound trout under my belt so happy enough with life, but rather down to be at home once more. Fortunately my Boathouse Lake patron allowed me a final six days at the water and between work, I fished there all I could. The weather, for once, was warm and I spent the third afternoon swimming – not really for pleasure but rather to check out my theory of 'hot' locations. After four hours in that lake, I can honestly say I have never been bitten so much in my entire life! Every leech, mosquito and swan mussel must have taken blood or skin and I felt ragged at the end. It was, however, worth the effort.

My theory about the hard, sandy areas was confirmed. I found some dozen of these amidst a general sea of mud and silt. All were quite large and overall the water was noticeably cooler as springs gushed in. They were also, I believed, definitely the areas where I had seen carp feed in the past.

I investigated the swim I had been fishing for two and a half days. A good many carp had used it to pass over but I had not as yet convinced one to stop and feed. The bed was very soft, slimy and silty. It was four feet deep. I ducked and searched around. In the silt itself I came across a mass of my own bait, sunk an inch or so down. Presumably the carp had not seen them and probably had not smelt them either. As it was obviously not an area they investigated thoroughly, I stood little or no chance of landing from that particular swim.

By the boathouse itself, I found two spring-cleared sand areas – one close to the alders and the second straight out at forty yards. Both could clearly be seen from the balcony. For two days I could not fish because of work, but I fed both each day, twice a day. On the sixth evening, I cast out at 7.00 p.m. and at 7.20 p.m. the indicator rose. A really good fish was on. After a thirty-yard run, it crashed out in the sun's reflection and doubled back to the right towards the alder fringe. Fast though I rewound, I could not keep a tight line. It hit the bottom trailing branches and all went solid. Young Simon had by now joined me and we knew it was gone. As a last hope on my last night, I took off my clothes once more and dropped my still-aching body back into the water. Rod held high, I half walked, half swam to the alders. I traced the line into the branches and, there, still, was my carp. It was quite docile now, its snout wedged in dead branches.

For half a minute I thought, then gently broke the worst of the woodwork around it. Now, hand on its nose, I turned the fish and gently backed her out into open water. She came lamb-like – until I tried to cradle her. She exploded. The water foamed. She was away and I was dragged after her into the swell.

For ten minutes more we fought it out. I was almost swimming and she was never more than five yards from me, often actually above me in the water. Oh, the glory of the pictures of that! Looking up to this fine fish silhouetted by the sunset, with the light pouring through her fins.

The end was climactic. She turned towards me, and in panic, blindly rushed at my chest. She swerved but caught me a blow, strong enough to rock me over. She too had turned belly up, the line caught under a pectoral. I righted myself, saw she was helpless, and gently led her to the net and Simon on the bank.

It was all over but for the weighing. She was massively long and broad but very sleek with it. She went low 'thirties' and was almost certainly the mid-thirty I believed I had lost earlier in the summer. It was altogether a magnificent moment.

With fish like these, or the ferox of John MacDonald, or the pike of Dan Leary, it does not matter how long you need to wait or whatever rigours you need undergo. Wild fish are worth every sacrifice and if you only get one a year, or one every two years – or even one a decade – you will be repaid for the effort. These really are one of angling's many pinnacles.

Without any fish at all, just to have been out in the wonderful Highlands, or the Welsh hills or a country estate would have been enough. There is a beauty in these places to be appreciated by all. I happened to be staying at the Foyers Hotel on Ness when I joined some Mancunians staying there. 'Have you ever seen the stars properly?' one of them asked his mate. 'They sweep end to end of the sky. They are magnificent. If you live in a city you never see them right. Only up here, in the wild, can you know them all . . . see all the constellations.'

Later, in the same bar, there was talk of the monster of the loch and pleasure that Deep Scan – the sonar attack on the beast – had failed. 'It's marvellous to think that there is something wild down there, untouched – untouchable like – unexploited by us all.'

But, of course, there were places and times less perfect. It happens, some nights, away for a month or two at a stretch, that you get your head down in the strangest of places. One April evening, we (Miller and I) were thrown out of our beloved Dick Down Hotel by a party of pre-booked hikers. A severe Highland frost was settling, making it too cold to sleep out or even stay in the car overnight. We were forced, therefore, to book into another inn, the closest to us, but still some forty miles away in another glen.

We fished as usual until nightfall, had a last meal in our base hotel, and set out across the hills at 10.00 p.m. The journey was exhilarating. The sky was brilliantly clear and star studded. All round, moonlight glowed from the snow-

The low 30lb landed at last. There was drama until the last moment.

[140]

capped peak and we passed the dark clusters of deer browsing on the moor. In the valleys beneath our winding road, the occasional lights of little lost crofts sparkled.

We dropped down from the heights, followed a silvery loch for some seven miles and came at last to the brightly-lit inn. The bar was a magnet to all around – foresters, crofters, shepherds and sportsmen and for a long while we enjoyed some spirited company. But we were dog-tired and asked at last to leave the party and be shown to our beds. It seemed that we were to sleep in a shack outhouse, which did not really concern us. Nor were we bothered by the sight of two rather decrepit bunk-beds. I climbed aloft, Miller sank below and within minutes we were goners to the world. I can even remember my dreams of giant ferox twisting and lungeing in deep willow green water and the sunlight ricocheting off the wave caps.

'My God! My God! Oh, my God! No! No! Hell! Hell and bastards! Oh no! My God!' I was wide awake. It was nearly 3.00 a.m. From the other side of the thin wooden wall it sounded as though the Furies themselves were loose. One man there was snoring and sneezing, both together, the one sound as loud as a hog and

the other as sharp as a thunder clap. His partner, though, was in some demented dream. The swearing grew worse, and, if possible, even louder. The Glaswegian accent became thicker as words dived deeper into depravity. On and on through the night the living horror continued without let or pause. It was grotesque. It was horrible, but little by little, Miller and I began to giggle out of our anger and then laugh until the tears streamed on to the pillows. We hammered on the walls. 'Give us a chance, lads.' But to no avail whatsoever. The two Scots next to us would have slept through hurricane, earthquake and nuclear war combined.

By 4.00 a.m., the man was screaming out 'Murder! Murder! Die, yer bastard. Watch the knife! Mac! The knife!' Miller and I were wondering what kind of mind was at work, what pit of a life was being exposed. But, as the first rays of dawn light broke, the nightmare ebbed away in a dying of yelling and even the snoring started to abate. At last we grabbed a couple of hours uneasy sleep before breakfast.

In the dining room, sparkling April sunshine danced off the cutlery and the smell of bacon rose both warm and crisp. At least we were eating well but, when the door was kicked open, a wicked sight tumbled into view. The Scot from the adjoining nightmare stumbled from table to wall and slumped down in a chair near us. He held his head in his hand and groaned constantly. He slurred 'Whisky, a large one', to the waitress. 'And quick with it, woman.'

'A bad night?' I asked him. He looked at me blankly. 'What d'ye mean, man?' 'Oh nothing really,' I was quick to add, 'just you don't look to have slept very well, that's all.' 'Slept like a baby,' he replied. 'Highland air sends me right off. I come up here for a damned good rest. You canna find peace like this in Glasgow...'

Miller and I decided then, on the spot, never to spend the night at that fair city!

But on reflection, Scotland was ever so. We were not the first English travellers to fall foul of a Scottish drinker. I quote from Dorothy Wordsworth's *Reflections of a Tour made in Scotland – 1803*. 'It came on a very stormy night. [Miller's and mine was icy clear]. The wind rattled every window in the house and it rained heavily. [There was not a breath of wind our night]. William (Wordsworth) and Coleridge (the poet of Ancient Mariner fame) had bad beds in a two-bedded room. [So did we]. And they were disturbed by a drunken man, who had come to the inn when we were gone to sleep.' It seems there is absolutely nothing new for the traveller, whether walker, poet or fisherman.